DRAGON BALL
FULL COLOR FREEZA ARC

3

STORY AND ART BY
AKIRA TORIYAMA

DRAGON BALL

FULL COLOR FREEZA ARC

CONTENTS

DRAGON BALL

FULL COLOR

FREEZA ARC

THIS DUDE REALLY *IS* PSYCHO. HE'S ABOUT TO BE KILLED AND HE'S SMILING!

HUH?

Chapter 035 • Super Saiyan?!

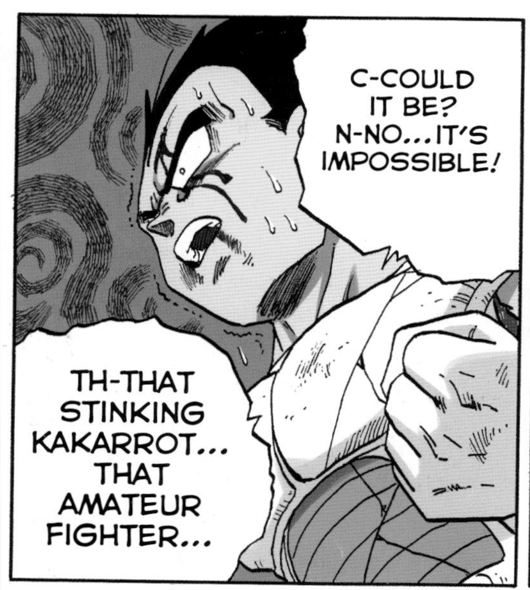
C-COULD IT BE? N-NO...IT'S IMPOSSIBLE!
TH-THAT STINKING KAKARROT... THAT AMATEUR FIGHTER...

SOME-THING'S STRANGE ...
GOKU NEVER USED TO BLUFF LIKE THAT...
DOESN'T HE SEE HOW POWER-FUL THIS GUY IS...?

H-HE COULD NEVER BECOME THE LEGENDARY SUPER SAIYAN...!!

I CAN'T HANDLE ANY MORE OF THIS LOSER'S JOKES...
IT'S TIME TO SHUT HIM UP—FOREVER!

THEY SAY A SUPER SAIYAN APPEARS ONLY ONCE IN A THOUSAND YEARS. I'VE ALWAYS SAID IT WAS JUST A MYTH... AND I WAS SURE THAT EVEN IF IT WERE POSSIBLE...

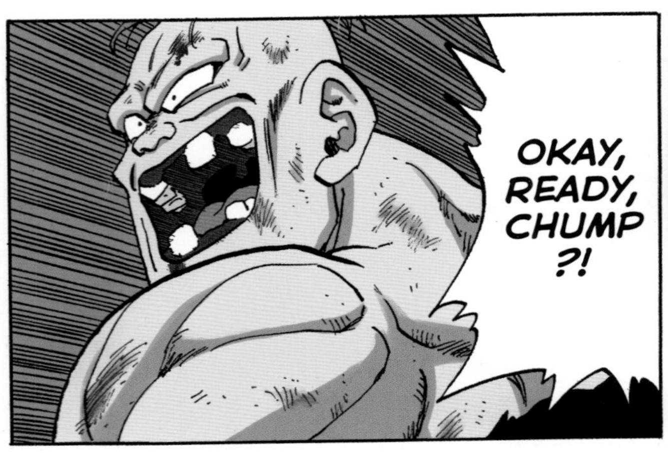
OKAY, READY, CHUMP ?!

...THE ONLY WARRIOR WHO COULD POSSIBLY BECOME ONE... WAS ME!

バッ
GINYU SPECIAL FORCE!

ATTACK!!

HUH
?!
WHA
?!

!!
UM...
?!

H-HE DIS-
APPEARED
!!
W-WHAT
...
HE'S NOT
ANYWHERE
!!

キッ

...

I DON'T
GET
THIS...
...?

pi
pi
pi

WHAT
?!

WHAT THE...?!

THAT BLASTED ...!!
WHEN DID HE...

H-HE'S ALL THE WAY OVER THERE...?!
!?

YOU WON'T HAVE TO GET HURT IF YOU LEAVE NOW.
...

YOU GUYS MUST BE MORE OF THAT CREEP FREEZA'S MEN.

WAFFFT
OH, RIGHT ...!!

TMP

Y-YOU THINK YOU'RE REAL FAST, HUH? WELL... HEH HEH...
YOU CAN'T WIN BY JUST RUNNING AWAY!

I-IT LOOKED LIKE VEGETA KNEW WHERE GOKU WAS... DID HE SEE SOMETHING...?!

わなわな...

GUESS I'VE GOT TO SHOW YOU MY ULTIMATE ATTACK, THEN!! MAY AS WELL WARN YOU—YOU CAN'T RUN FROM THIS!!

'CAUSE A WHOLE BIG WIDE CIRCLE AROUND ME JUST GETS BLOWN TO NOTHHHH-THING!

ULTRA ...

MEGA...

NNN... NGH...
SORRY.
YOU WERE SO WIDE OPEN, I COULDN'T HELP MYSELF.

Y-Y...
YOU... PUNK...
ガク
ガク

ズーーーーン

!!
WHA...?!

IT CAN'T BE...
N-N-NO WAY...
D-DID DAD... BEAT HIM...?
...HUH ...?
twitch
twitch

THAT ATTACK... SHOULDN'T HAVE DONE ANYTHING...
IT WAS SOME SORT OF TRICK...

E-EVEN IF HE CAUGHT HIM OFF GUARD ...
THAT GUY NEVER EVEN FLINCHED AT ANY OF VEGETA'S OR OUR ATTACKS... AND THAT WAS JUST ONE BLOW...

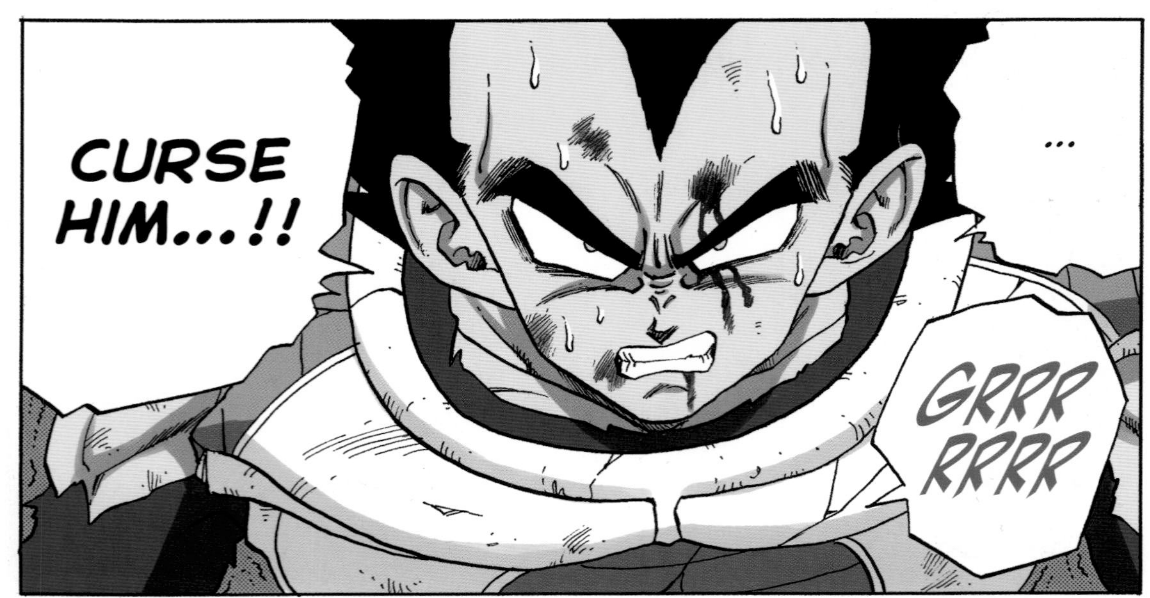

...
CURSE HIM...!!
GRRR RRRR

THAT WAS NO TRICK... IT WAS NO TECHNIQUE...
IT WAS JUST ONE... TREMENDOUS BLOW!

HE'S UTTERLY SURPASSED SAIYAN STRENGTH...
WHAT KIND OF TRAINING DID HE DO...?
...HE'S A COMPLETELY DIFFERENT WARRIOR FROM THE ONE I FOUGHT ON EARTH...
IS THE LEGEND TRUE...?!

IS HE THE SUPER SAIYAN?!

TWITCH

TWITCH

Chapter 036 • Jheese and Butta

HEAR THAT, BUTTA? THIS FOOL'S TALKIN' IN HIS SLEEP AGAIN!

HE SEEMS TO BE UNDER THE IMPRESSION THAT HE BESTED REACOOM BY HIS OWN POWER.

WHEN IT MUST HAVE BEEN ONLY THE COMBINATION OF FREAKISH LUCK AND REACOOM LETTING HIS GUARD DOWN...

LET'S GO!!

ATTACK!!

TAH !!
TAH !!

NOW YOU'LL SEE WHAT HAPPENS WHEN YOU UNDER-ESTIMATE THE GINYU F–

WHA–?!!
R-R-RRRG ...!!

Y-YOU... LOUSY ...!!
KST

YOU KEEP LEAVING YOUR-SELVES WIDE OPEN.

SAY WHAT ?!!
HAH !!

HYAH!!

キッ

キッ

W-WHAT IN THE...?!
W-WHAT DID HE JUST DO...?!

I-IT WAS A *KIAI* ...
H-HE BLEW THEM AWAY... WITH A BASIC LITTLE *KIAI*...

B-BUT ...
I THOUGHT THESE GUYS WERE REAL STRONG ...?
TH-THEY'RE HELPLESS AGAINST DAD...

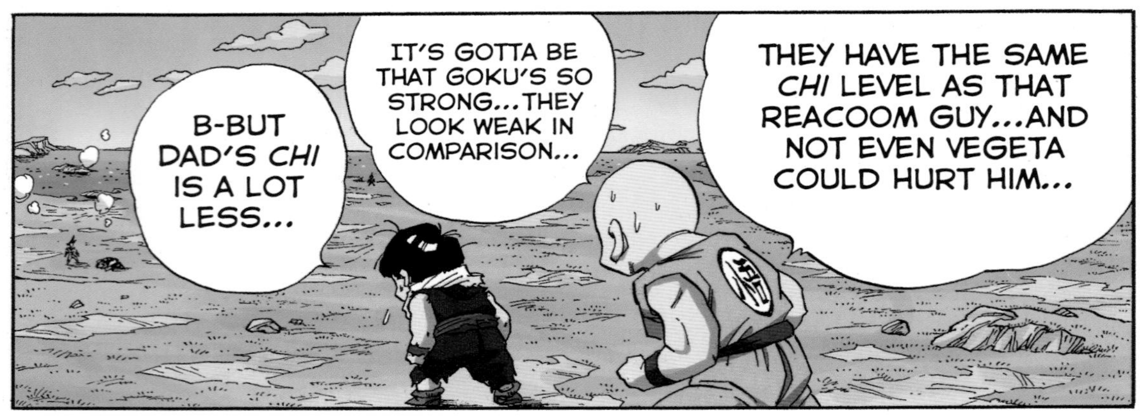
THEY HAVE THE SAME CHI LEVEL AS THAT REACOOM GUY...AND NOT EVEN VEGETA COULD HURT HIM...
IT'S GOTTA BE THAT GOKU'S SO STRONG...THEY LOOK WEAK IN COMPARISON...
B-BUT DAD'S CHI IS A LOT LESS...

W-WHAT THE HECK IS GOING ON?
HIS BATTLE STRENGTH STILL ISN'T A BIT OVER 5,000!

HE'S RADICALLY RAISING HIS CHI ONLY IN THE INSTANT HE ATTACKS...
SO INSTAN-TANEOUSLY THAT NOT EVEN THE SCOUTERS CAN PICK IT UP...CON-SERVING HIS ENERGY, NO DOUBT...

BUT THE POWER IT TAKES TO DO THAT...
HOW DID HE GET SO MUCH POWER...?!

NOW I'M ANNOYED!! I REFUSE TO LET THIS INSIGNIFICANT INSECT MAKE A FOOL OUT OF ME!!
JHEESE—CAN YOU HEAR ME? USE YOUR CRUSHER BALL!! WITH HIS SPEED, HE'LL DODGE IT, OF COURSE...

HMPH...I CAN'T BELIEVE WE GOTTA GO THROUGH ALL THIS FOR THAT SPECK OF DIRT...
GOTCHA.

ISN'T IT OBVIOUS?! I'LL SMASH HIM FROM BEHIND AS HE DODGES IT!! NO MATTER HOW FAST HE IS, I'M STILL THE FASTEST IN THE UNIVERSE!
SO WHY DO IT?

!!
!!

CRUSHER

BALL!!

HEH

JUST TRY AND MOVE!!

WHY AREN'T YOU DODGING?!!

W-WHAT ARE DOING?!

NO!!
HE-
HE DE-FLECTED IT!!
UGH!!!
IT...
...CAN-NOT BE!!
EH?!
WHA-WHAT?!

DRAGON BALL

WHAT'S EVERYONE DOING? DID THEY FORGET ABOUT ME AND THEY'RE JUST PLAYING AROUND?
SHEESH. ALWAYS WASTING MY TIME LIKE THIS IS BAD FOR MY SKIN.

Chapter 037 • With Allies Like These…

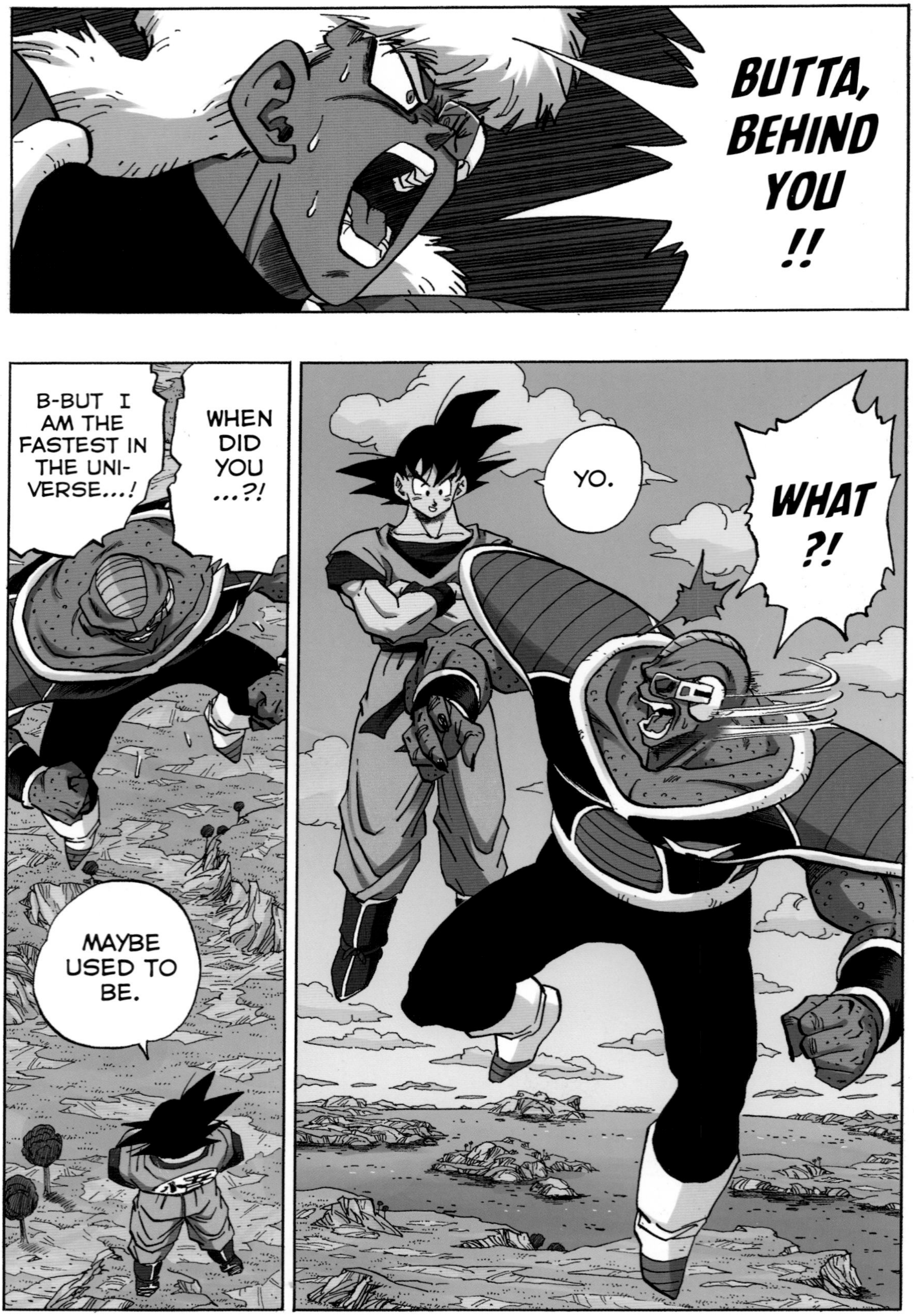

UNBELIEV-
ABLE...NOT
ONLY DID
HE DE-
FLECT MY
CRUSHER
BALL...
...B-BUT HE
TOOK BUTTA'S
BACK...THIS
IS LIKE A
NIGHTMARE...

THEY
TELL
ME...
...I'M A
SAIYAN,
RAISED
ON
EARTH.

WHA...
WHAT
ARE
YOU...?

I
WOULDN'T
KNOW
ABOUT
THAT.
I DID DO
SOME
PRETTY
COOL
TRAIN-
ING,
THOUGH.
BAH!! NO
SAIYAN
COULD BE
THAT FAST!!

RUN ALL YOU WANT, FOOL!!

TAH!!

TAAH!!

ENOUGH OF THIS!!
NOBODY MAKES THE GINYU FORCE LOOK STUPID!!

WHOA!

HSH
HSH
HSH

YOU WANT ME TO SHOW YOU—
THAT I'M NOT JUST FAST?!

!?
HYAH !!

TWITCH
TWITCH

ズ・・・ン
UHHH...

DO YOU UNDERSTAND NOW?! THERE'S NO POINT IN FIGHTING!! JUST TAKE YOUR FRIENDS AND GET OFF THIS PLANET BEFORE YOU END UP DEAD!!

...N... NNNH...

...

W-WHAT ARE YOU DOING, FOOL?!
FINISH HIM!!

HE IS FINISHED.
THERE'S NO REASON TO KILL HIM!
HRRR...

H-HOW... IS THIS...H-HAPPENING ...?
W-WE'RE... C-CAPTAIN GINYU'S... SPECIAL FORCE...
W-WE'RE THE ELITE...OF THE ELITE...THE FIVE FINEST... WARRIORS IN... THE ENTIRE UNIVERSE... H-HOW COULD THAT STUPID... LOW-POWERED...

IT...IS A NIGHT-MARE...
...ME... DEFEATED... HELPLESS...

I WON'T TAKE IT!!
バシュッ
HEY! H-HE RAN AWAY...!!

HUH ...
AND HE LEFT HIS FRIENDS ...

H-HEY... ARE YOU REALLY ...?
...GOKU ...?
...

WHAT ?!

VEGETA!!
WHAT ARE YOU -?!

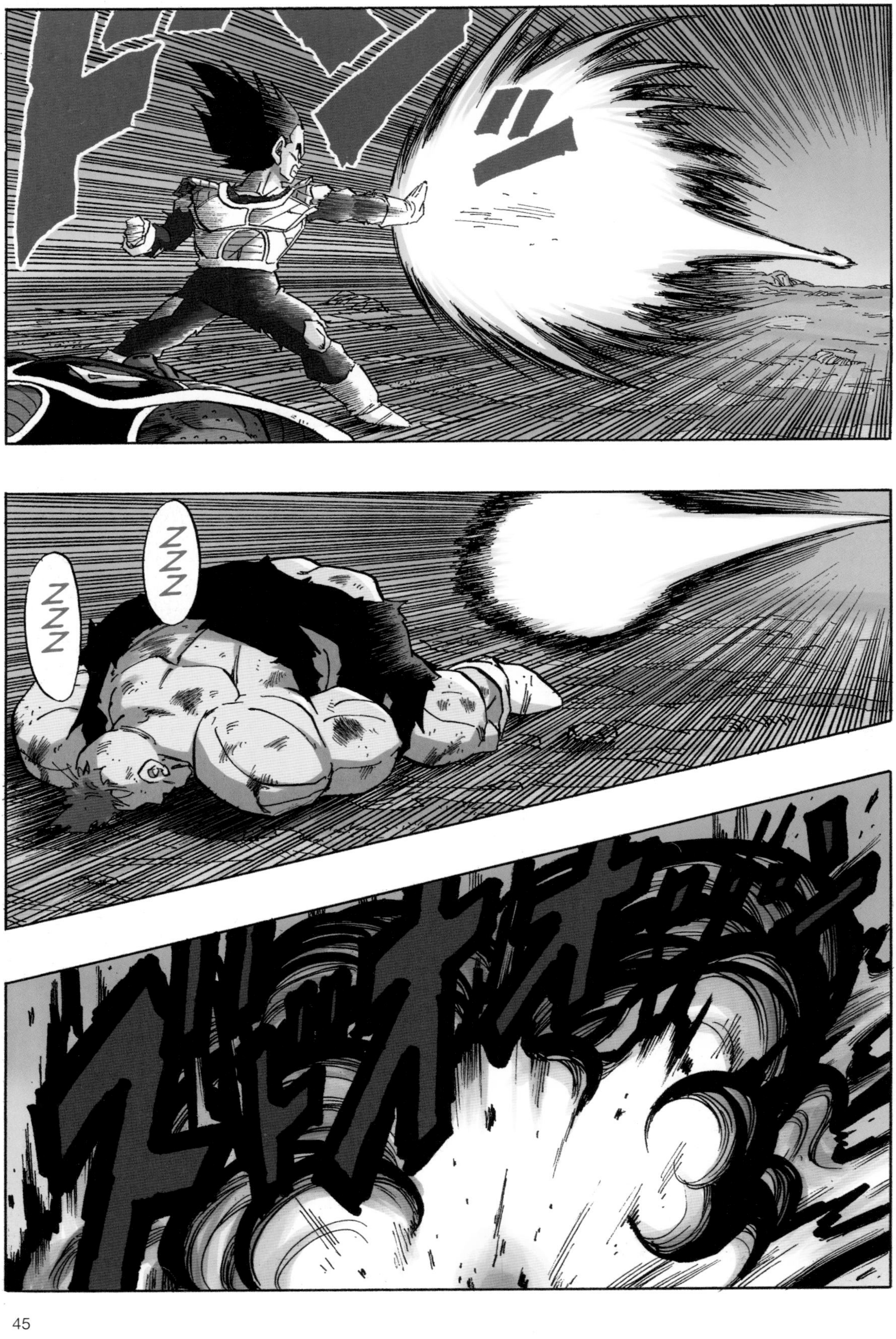

ZZZ

ZZZ

ゴゴゴ...

I SAID THERE WAS NO REASON TO KILL ANYBODY!!
THEY COULDN'T EVEN MOVE!!

YOUR SOFTNESS MAKES ME RETCH, AS USUAL...
WHY DID YOU STAND THERE AND LET ONE GET AWAY?! YOU COULD'VE FINISHED HIM OFF EASILY!!

YOU'RE NO SUPER SAIYAN AFTER ALL...

"SUPER SAIYAN" ...?

...

THERE IT IS...HEH HEH HEH...

Chapter 038 • Ginyu Steps In

WAIT A MINUTE... I'M MORE POWERFUL THAN EVER...BY FAR!
AND YOU'RE SAYING I *STILL* DON'T MATCH UP AGAINST FREEZA?!
FREEZA'S MIGHT IS BEYOND ANYTHING YOU CAN CONCEIVE. YOU CANNOT EVEN PREPARE YOURSELF.

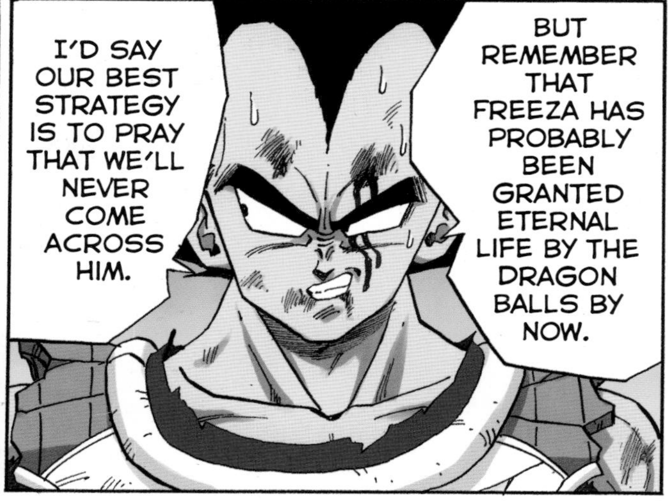

BUT REMEMBER THAT FREEZA HAS PROBABLY BEEN GRANTED ETERNAL LIFE BY THE DRAGON BALLS BY NOW.
I'D SAY OUR BEST STRATEGY IS TO PRAY THAT WE'LL NEVER COME ACROSS HIM.

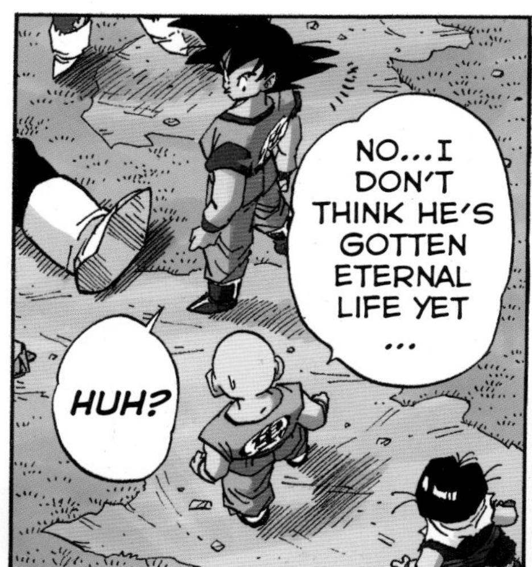

NO...I DON'T THINK HE'S GOTTEN ETERNAL LIFE YET ...
HUH?

WHAT ?!
HOW DO YOU KNOW ?!

IF THESE DRAGON BALLS ARE THE SAME AS THE ONES ON EARTH, IT SHOULD GET *DARK* WHEN SHENLONG APPEARS, RIGHT?!
BUT IT'S BEEN LIGHT ALL ALONG! I D-DON'T THINK IT'S HAP-PENED YET...

... SHEN-LONG? ...?!
YOU MEAN... THERE'S SOME SORT OF BEING INVOLVED WITH THESE DRAGON BALLS?!

I GET IT!! HE DOESN'T KNOW THE WORDS!
HE THINKS YOU GET YOUR WISH JUST BY GETTING ALL SEVEN BALLS!!
WE STILL HAVE A CHANCE TO GET *OUR* WISH!!

"THE WORDS ..."?!
BUT... WHAT...?
WE CAN STILL BRING EVERYBODY BACK TO LIFE!!
YAH!!

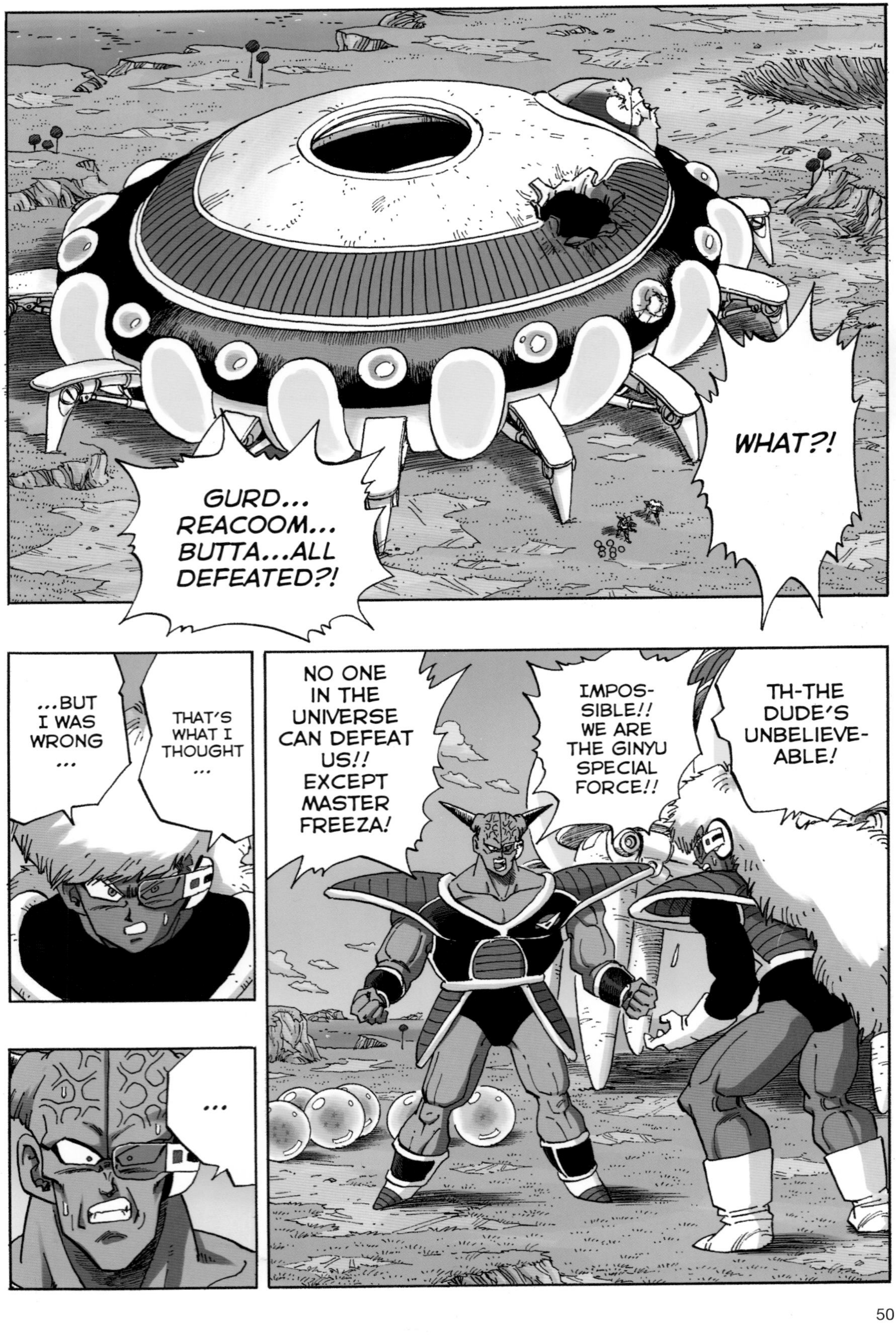

GURD... REACOOM... BUTTA...ALL DEFEATED?!

WHAT?!

BLAST IT...
THEN IT WASN'T A SCOUTER MALFUNCTION THAT MADE THEIR POWER SEEM TO DISAPPEAR...

SH-SHOULD WE TELL MASTER FREEZA ...?
AND HUMILIATE OURSELVES IN FRONT OF HIM?! DON'T BE STUPID!!

WHEW... IT'S A GOOD THING HE WAS AWAY...
NOW, ALLOW *ME* TO SHOW YOU HOW TO FIGHT!

JHEESE—HIDE THE DRAGON BALLS. MASTER FREEZA WILL BE MOST DISPLEASED IF THEY DISAPPEAR.
Y-YES SIR.

STOMP
STOMP

GINYU SPECIAL FORCE-GO!!

I BURIED 'EM. NOBODY'LL FIND THE THINGS NOW.
ALL RIGHT, THEN! THIS FOOL NEEDS A LESSON FROM CAPTAIN GINYU!

WELL, I DON'T KNOW WHO THIS CHUMP IS...
BUT HE'S REALLY IN FOR IT NOW!!

...
SOME-HOW THE SPECIAL FIGHTING POSE JUST DOESN'T CUT IT WHEN THERE ARE ONLY TWO OF US ...

ドヒュン
ドヒュン

NOW WE'VE JUST GOTTA GET THE DRAGON BALLS BACK...
VEGETA... YOU KNOW THESE GUYS. ANY GOOD IDEAS?

I THOUGHT YOU WERE GOING TO FIGHT FREEZA.

WELL...I WANT TO! BUT...TO TELL THE TRUTH, THE LORD OF THE WORLDS TOLD ME NOT TO FIGHT HIM TOO...
I THINK FIRST I'D BETTER BRING THE GUYS YOU KILLED ON EARTH BACK TO LIFE.

THAT'S YOUR *WISH?!* IDIOT! WHAT GOOD WILL IT BE WHEN FREEZA BLOWS UP THE WHOLE PLANET SOMEDAY?
GIVE ME ETERNAL LIFE INSTEAD.

NO WAY!! IF WE DO THAT YOU'D BE NO DIFFERENT THAN FREEZA!!
EH?!

TWO CHI HEADING THIS WAY...
OF COURSE. JHEESE, THE ONE YOU LET GET AWAY... IS BRINGING CAPTAIN GINYU!
I WONDER IF EVEN YOU CAN HANDLE HIM?

H-HE'S RIGHT, GOKU!! THIS IS TROUBLE ...!!

WAIT... WHERE'S FREEZA ?!
HE WAS AT THE SPACESHIP WHERE GINYU TOOK THE DRAGON BALLS...

I FEEL A POWERFUL CHI FAR OFF THAT WAY...THAT MUST BE FREEZA...
HUH?!

I GET IT NOW!! FREEZA COULDN'T GET HIS WISH—SO HE'S GOING TO MAKE A NAMEKIAN TELL HIM WHAT TO DO!!

THAT'S WHERE THE GREAT ELDER IS!!
OH NO!!
B-BUT THAT'S THE DIREC-TION...

HE DOESN'T KNOW THAT THE DRAGON BALLS WILL DISAPPEAR IF THE GREAT ELDER DIES!!
H-HE'LL KILL THE GREAT ELDER AFTER HE FINDS OUT HOW TO GET HIS WISH!!

WHAT? SO THERE WERE MORE NAMEKIANS IN THAT HOUSE?!
IS THAT WHO MADE THE DRAGON BALLS HERE?!
YEAH!! OH, MAN!! THIS IS BAD!!

UNH ...!!

W-
WHAT ?!

SO YOU THOUGHT YOU MADE FOOLS OF US, HUH? WELL, NOW YOU'LL FIND OUT WHO THE FOOLS ARE— FOOLS!!

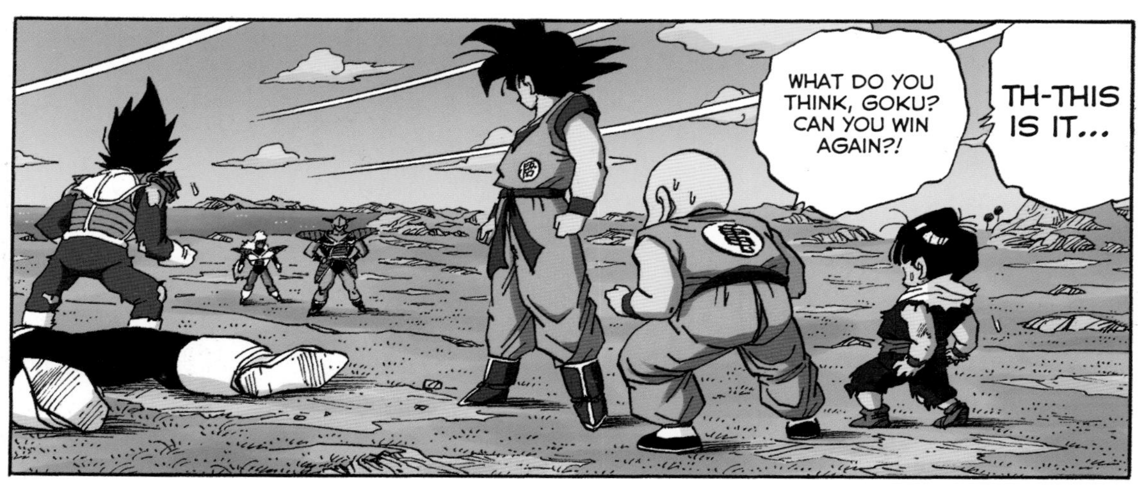
WHAT DO YOU THINK, GOKU? CAN YOU WIN AGAIN?!
TH-THIS IS IT...

HIS POWER IS ONLY 5,000...
THIS IS HIM...?

I WON'T KNOW UNTIL I TRY.
THIS CAPTAIN GUY DOES LOOK A LOT TOUGHER THAN THE REST...

DO YOU ALWAYS BELIEVE EVERYTHING YOU READ?!
HE MUST BE ABLE TO SUP-PRESS AND INCREASE HIS POWER INSTANTA-NEOUSLY!

YEAH! THAT'S WHAT'S SO CRAZY!
IDIOT!

IT'S NOT IMPOSSIBLE.
HE MUST BE A MUTATION LIKE US...BORN AS A GIFTED FIGHTER.

I ESTIMATE HIS TRUE POWER TO BE AROUND 60,000...
60,000?! H-HE'S A SAIYAN!! NO SAIYAN EVER GOT NEAR 60,000!!

WELL... THIS MAY BE THE BATTLE I'VE BEEN WAITING FOR...
THE FIRST BATTLE WHEN I CAN FINALLY USE MY FULL POWERS!

I'LL KEEP HIM BUSY.
YOU GO FOR THE DRAGON BALLS WITH THE RADAR! I'LL BET THEY LEFT THEM BY THE SPACESHIP.
IF I BEAT THIS GUY, I'LL COME JOIN YOU.

O-OKAY!
WE GOTTA HURRY OR THE GREAT ELDER'LL BE KILLED!
H-HE COULD ALREADY BE DEAD ...!

HURRY!

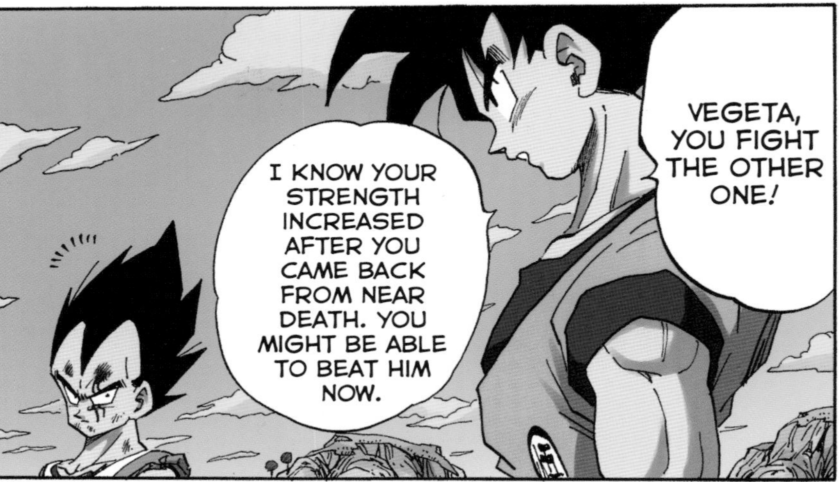
VEGETA, YOU FIGHT THE OTHER ONE!
I KNOW YOUR STRENGTH INCREASED AFTER YOU CAME BACK FROM NEAR DEATH. YOU MIGHT BE ABLE TO BEAT HIM NOW.

HEH... SO YOU KNEW...

R-REALLY ...?
...

ALL RIGHT!! GO!!
AND BE CAREFUL !!

GOOD LUCK, GOKU !!
バシュ
バシュッ
TH-THEY RAN AWAY ...!!
FORGET ABOUT THE SMALL FRY.

ALL RIGHT! HERE WE GO!!

AN OPENING!!!

Chapter 039 • A Matter of Pride

FFT
TMP
ギュルルルッ
HYAH!!
ブンッ
ザッ
シャッ
バッバババッ
イイイイイッ
シャシャシャッ

バッ
バッ

タッ
タッ

OW!
AARRGH... THAT JERK, VEGETA...

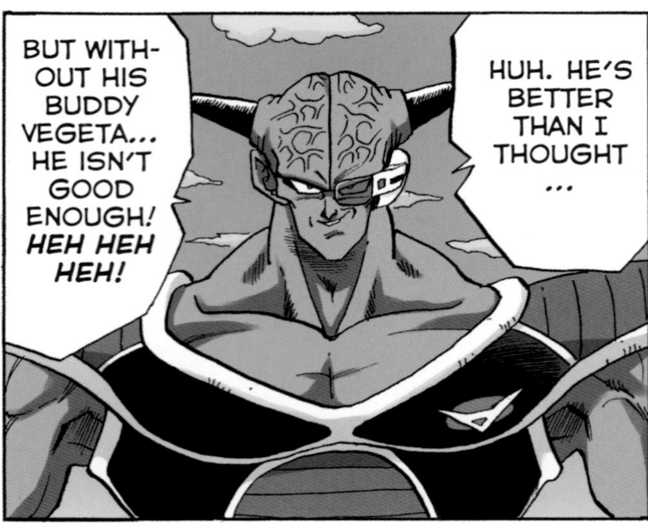
HUH. HE'S BETTER THAN I THOUGHT...
BUT WITH-OUT HIS BUDDY VEGETA... HE ISN'T GOOD ENOUGH! *HEH HEH HEH!*

HE'S GONNA MAKE ME FIGHT THESE GUYS WHILE HE RUNS OFF AND TAKES THE DRAGON BALLS FOR HIMSELF!
WELL, I BETTER SETTLE THIS QUICKLY THEN, OR OUR LAST HOPE IS GONE...

HA! THAT WAS EASY! I ESTIMATE THAT KAKARROT AND GINYU'S CAPABILITIES ARE PRACTICALLY THE SAME...
IF IT GOES WELL, THEY MIGHT ELIMINATE EACH OTHER! AND THAT'S ALL GOOD FOR ME!

HA HA HA! AFTER I BEAT THE INVOCATION OUT OF THOSE BRATS, I'LL FINISH THEM OFF!
THEN I'LL BECOME IMMORTAL— AND I'LL FINALLY HAVE A CHANCE AGAINST FREEZA!!

ALL RIGHT. SORRY TO HAVE TO DO THIS AFTER YOU JUST SHOWED UP, BUT I'M GONNA HAVE TO FINISH THIS QUICK.
HA HA HA! LISTEN TO YOU! THAT'S THE FIRST TIME ANYONE'S EVER SAID SOMETHING LIKE THAT TO ME!

YOU SEE, I HAPPEN TO BE ABLE TO CHANGE MY BATTLE STRENGTH AT WILL, TOO!
I ALMOST REGRET HAVING TO BEAT THAT CONFIDENCE OUT OF YOU!

BUT HEY, WHY NOT? EVEN IF THAT DUDE'S POWER REALLY DOES TO GO 60,000...
THE CAPTAIN'S MAXIMUM POWER MAKES THAT LOOK LIKE NOTHIN'!!

MAN... CAPTAIN GINYU IS SO COOL...

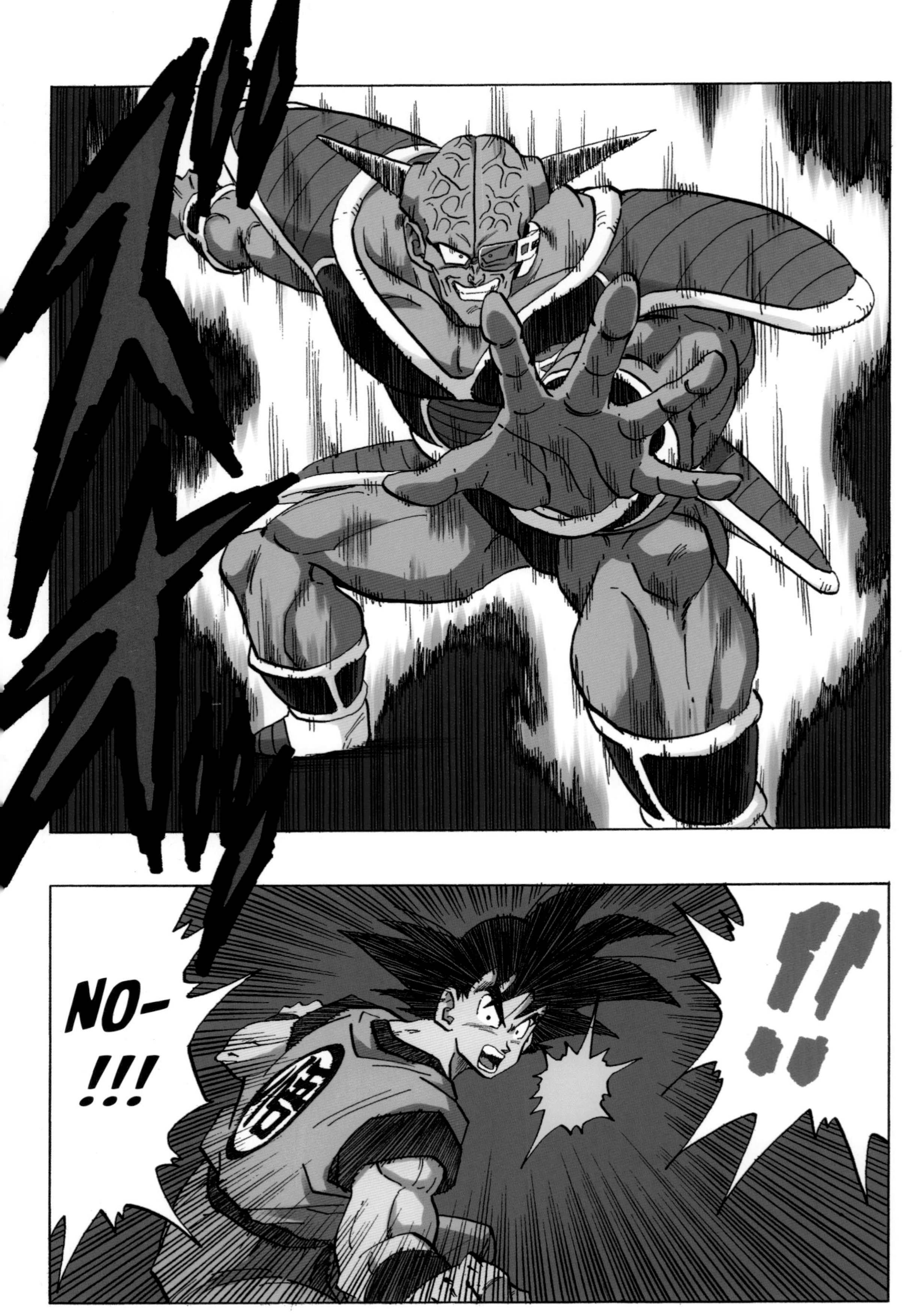
NO-
!!!
!!
!!

パァーーン
ドズゥ…ン

FSH

FFFT
HYOH!!

!!

EVEN FASTER THAN ME—!!

HE'S FAST!!

UH?!
NNKH!!!
!!
HA HA HA !!
I STOPPED HIM!!

CAPTAIN!! HE'S OURS!!
FINISH HIM!! BREAK HIS BACK!!

OHH... NO...!!
NNN... NNGH...!!

SO...S-STRONG! I CAN'T GET LOOSE!!
N-NO...CHOICE!! GOTTA USE...THE KAIÓ-KEN...!!

すっ…
!!

WHA...?!

C-CAPTAIN?!

WHO ASKED *YOU* TO HELP, FOOL?!
IF YOU INTERFERE AGAIN— *YOU'LL* BE THE ONE I FINISH!!

...

AS FOR *YOU*—!

DID YOU REALLY THINK I WOULDN'T NOTICE THAT YOU'RE CONCEALING YOUR TRUE STRENGTH?!
WHAT, ARE YOU SAVING IT UNTIL YOU MEET MASTER FREEZA? YOU WON'T GO VERY FAR BY UNDERESTIMATING ME!!
I DON'T OFTEN GET TO ENJOY MY BATTLES— SO GET SERIOUS AND FIGHT!

OKAY...
I'LL SHOW YOU MY FULL POWER, THEN...

THAT'S BETTER.
HOW COULD YOU DIE IN PEACE KNOWING YOU DIDN'T GIVE IT YOUR ALL?!

LOOK AT THAT THING, AND WATCH MY POWER READING...

I DON'T NEED ANY STINKING SCOUTER. I ALREADY FIGURED YOU OUT FOR ABOUT 85,000.

KAIÓ-KEN!!

HAIYAAAAAA!!

ゴゴゴゴ

pi pi pi

90,000 ...?!
100,000... 110,000... ?!

TH-THIS IS IMPOSSIBLE...
IT'S STILL INCREASING!

Chapter 040 • The Last Three Namekians

120,000...

130,000...
140,000...!!

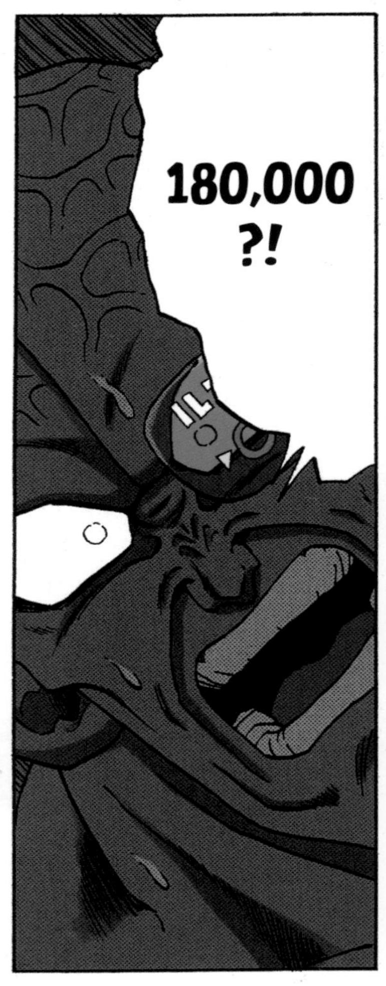
180,000
?!

IS THIS REAL?!
IS THIS... YOUR POWER ...?!

N-NO WONDER HE CREAMED US...
EVEN THE CAPTAIN'S TOP STRENGTH IS 120,000...
BUT... HOW COULD A SAIYAN C-COME THIS FAR...?!

LET ME TELL YOU JUST ONE MORE THING...
THIS IS NOTHING COMPARED TO WHEN I USE MY POWER IN BURSTS!

B... BURSTS...
PHEW...

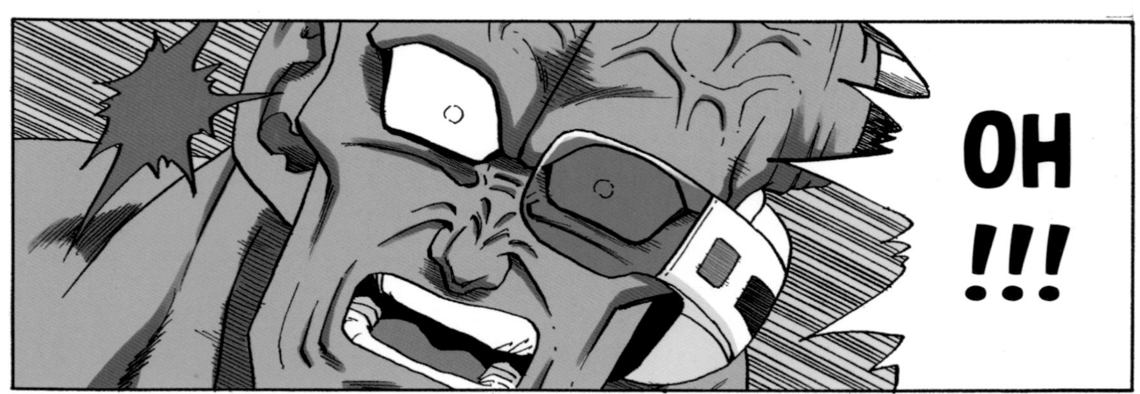
OH!!!

YOU... YOU MUST BE... THE LEGEND...!
THE SUPER SAIYAN!!

?!
VEGETA SAID SOME-THING ABOUT THAT TOO...
I WISH SOME-BODY WOULD EXPLAIN IT...

THE MIGHTIEST WARRIOR... IN THE COSMOS ?!
THE... SUPER SAIYAN ...?!

RRAUGH!!
HOW COULD THIS BE?!!

THE... THE ONLY THING...
...THAT MASTER FREEZA HIMSELF EVER FEARED ?!

DO YOU SEE? YOU CAN'T WIN.
I DON'T WANT TO WASTE TIME FIGHTING.
YOU'D BETTER LEAVE THIS PLANET.

YOU DON'T SEEM LIKE AS BAD A GUY AS THOSE OTHERS. I DON'T WANT TO KILL YOU.
W-WHAT ...?!
ARE YOU SERIOUS?!

YOU DON'T WANT TO WASTE TIME FIGHTING?! YOU DON'T WANT TO KILL ME?!
THE LEGEND OF THE SUPER SAYIAN HOLDS THAT HE WILL LOVE BLOODSHED AND BATTLE ABOVE ALL!

YOU... YOU'RE NO SUPER SAIYAN!!
YOU MAY HAVE TRIED TO BECOME ONE—BUT YOU'VE FAILED!!

...?

YOU ARE STRONGER THAN ME, I'LL GIVE YOU THAT...
BUT THAT'S WHAT I'VE WAITED FOR... *HEH HEH HEH...*

I SEE...
SO THE ONLY NAMEKIANS LEFT ARE THE THREE IN THERE ...

HE HAS FINALLY FOUND THIS PLACE...
HE IS ALMOST HERE...

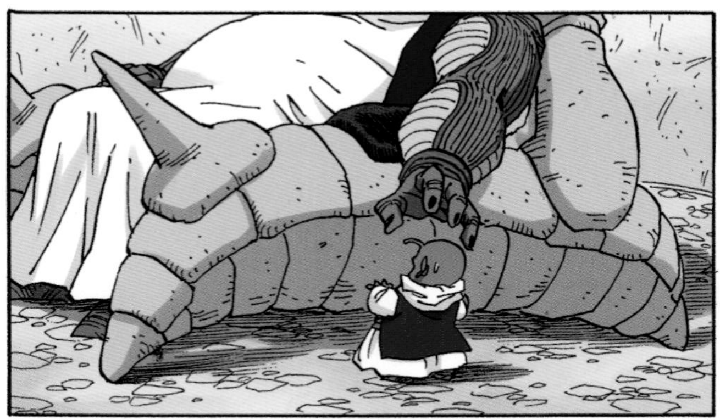

... OH...
...OH MY...

GO, DENDE...
THOSE PEOPLE FROM EARTH NEED YOU...I HAVE DRAWN OUT YOUR LATENT POWER...YOU SHOULD BE ABLE TO GET THERE QUICKLY...

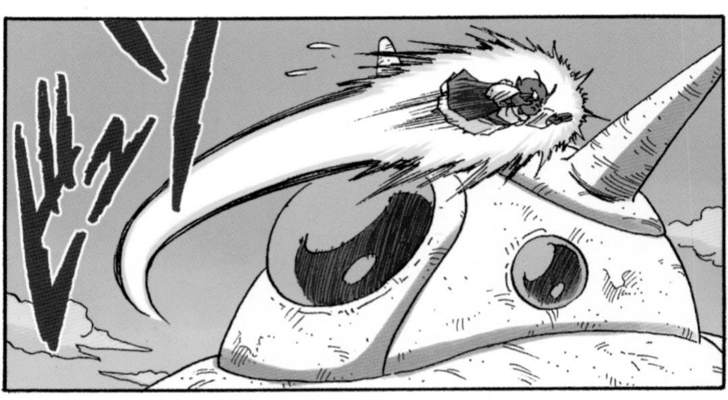

IT IS ONLY A QUESTION OF TIME... WHETHER I'M SLAIN FIRST...OR SIMPLY DIE OF OLD AGE...

HSST

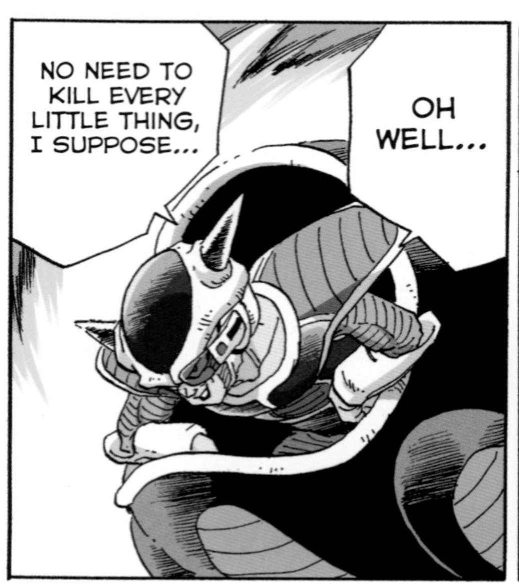
NO NEED TO KILL EVERY LITTLE THING, I SUPPOSE...
OH WELL...

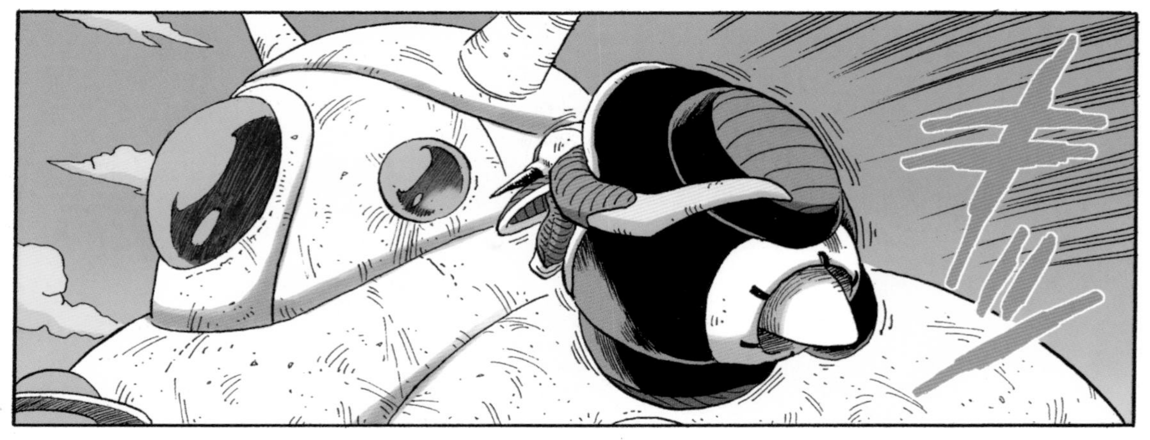

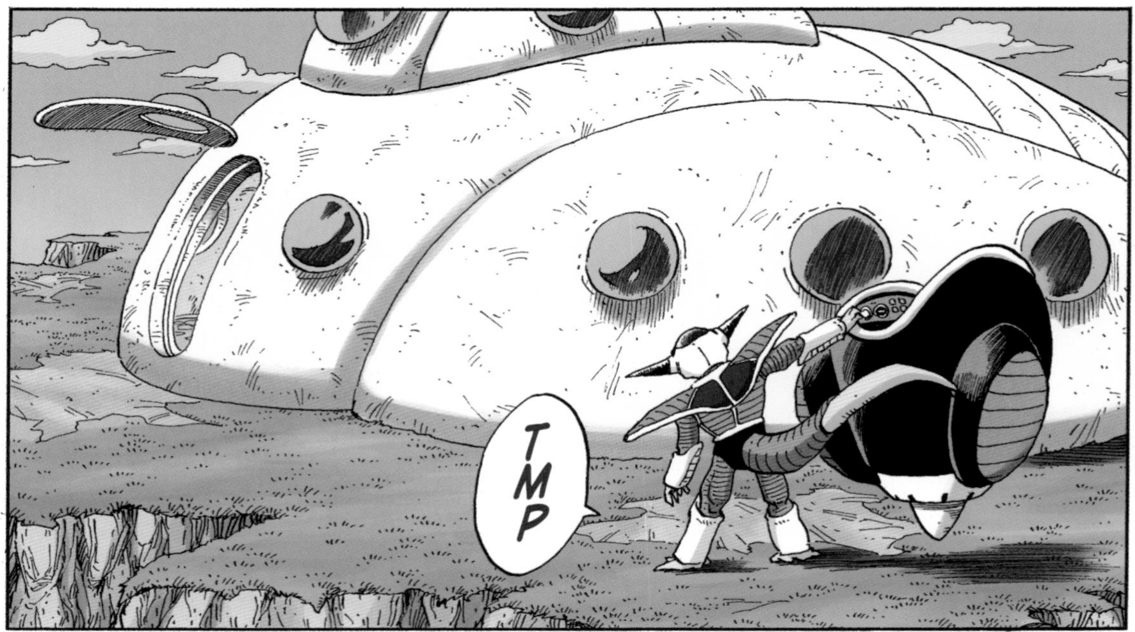
TMP

MAY I HELP YOU?

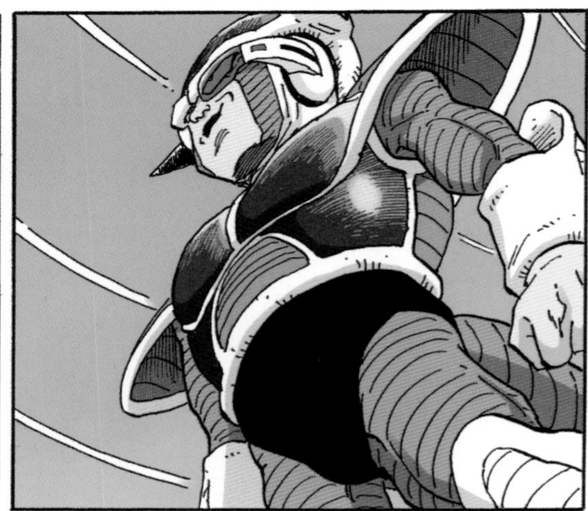

MY NAME IS FREEZA, AND I WANT MY WISH GRANTED BY YOUR DRAGON BALLS.
I'VE GATHERED ALL SEVEN BALLS, BUT I DON'T KNOW WHAT TO DO NEXT.

I WANT YOU TO TELL ME.
HOW DO I GET MY WISH?

I MUST ASK YOU TO LEAVE.
I CANNOT TELL ONE WHO IS EVIL.

I THINK IT IS TO YOUR BENEFIT TO BE HONEST. THERE ARE TWO OF YOU, ARE THERE NOT? I CAN GET IT OUT OF EITHER ONE OF YOU. IT WOULD REQUIRE NO EFFORT TO KILL YOU.
THEN DO SO...

THE ONE INSIDE IS THE GREAT ELDER OF PLANET NAMEK. IT WAS HE WHO CREATED THE DRAGON BALLS...
BUT LET ME WARN YOU BEFORE WE FIGHT.

AND IT IS HIS ENERGY THAT SUSTAINS THEM! KILL HIM—AND THE DRAGON BALLS WILL DISAPPEAR AS WELL!

OH-HO!

THE GREAT ELDER ...?

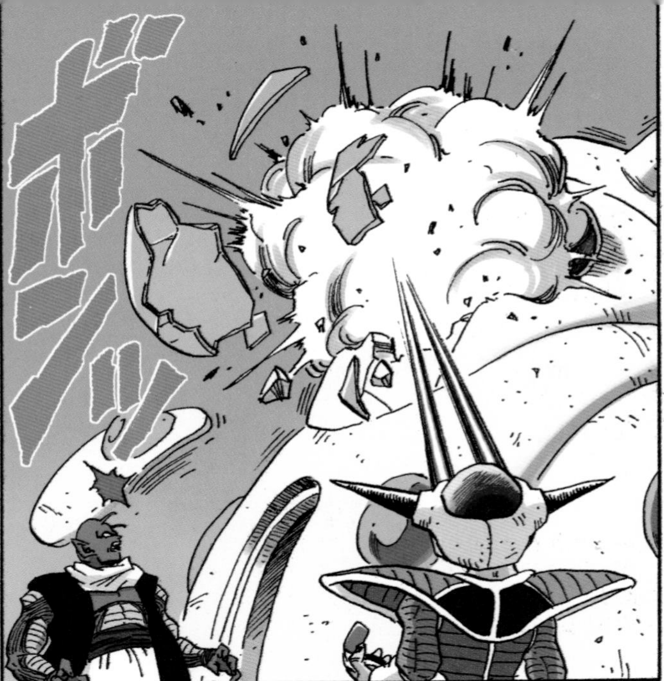

WHA ...?!

スッ・・・
!

INDEED...I THINK IT MAY BE TRUE...
HE IS CERTAINLY DIFFER-ENT FROM THE OTHER NAMEK-IANS...

GREAT ELDER...I ASSUME YOU HAVE NO INTENTION OF TELLING ME EITHER?
BUT SURELY YOU COULD NOT KEEP QUIET IF THIS MAN WERE ABOUT TO BE KILLED...

YOU WILL FIND NAIL UNLIKE THE OTHER NAMEKIANS YOU HAVE MURDERED.
AMONG ALL OF US, HE IS OUR LONE TRUE WARRIOR.
HE WILL NOT BE DEFEATED AS EASILY AS YOU IMAGINE.

...
SO YOU STILL WON'T TELL ME...

I LEAVE IT TO YOU, NAIL...BUY AS MUCH TIME AS YOU CAN...

I UNDER-STAND.

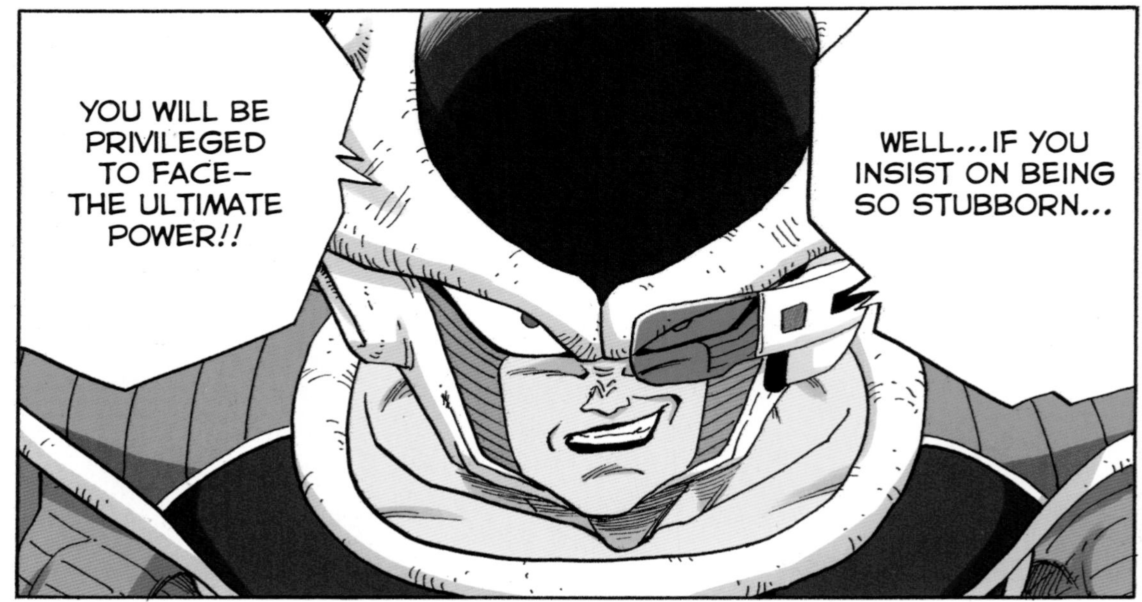
WELL...IF YOU INSIST ON BEING SO STUBBORN...
YOU WILL BE PRIVILEGED TO FACE— THE ULTIMATE POWER!!

Chapter 041 • Nail, Champion of Namek

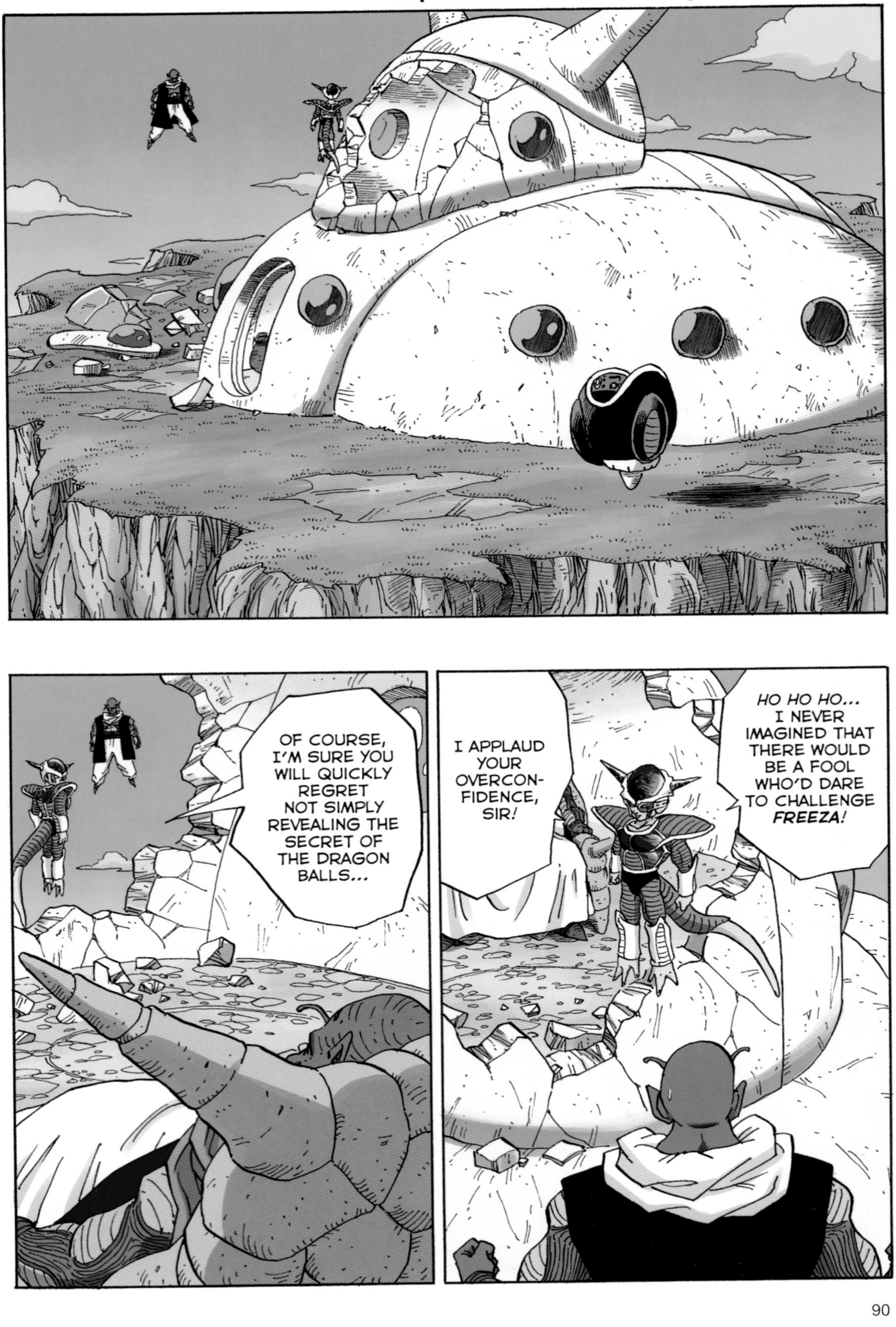

...WHEN YOU HAVE TO GASP IT OUT IN AGONY!

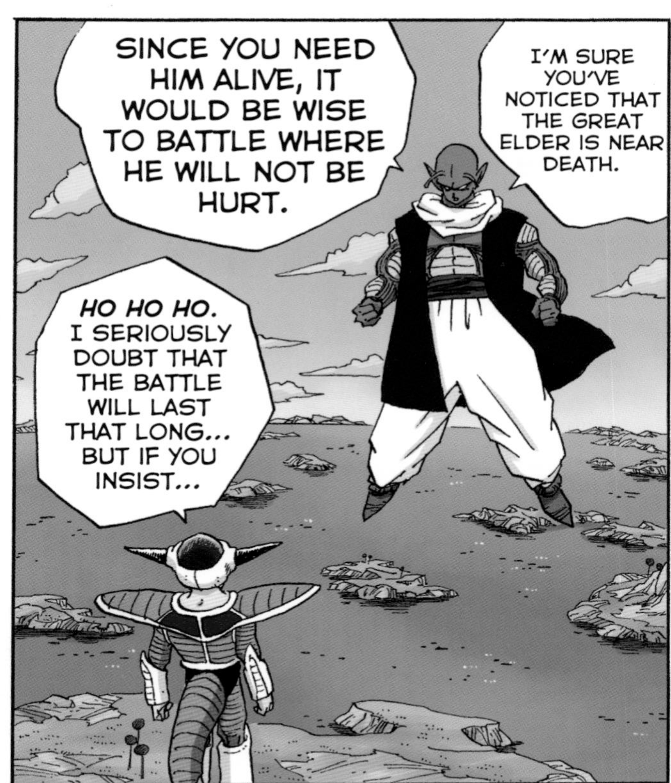
I'M SURE YOU'VE NOTICED THAT THE GREAT ELDER IS NEAR DEATH.
SINCE YOU NEED HIM ALIVE, IT WOULD BE WISE TO BATTLE WHERE HE WILL NOT BE HURT.
HO HO HO. I SERIOUSLY DOUBT THAT THE BATTLE WILL LAST THAT LONG... BUT IF YOU INSIST...

VN
VN

I'M SORRY, NAIL...YOU MUST HOLD OUT AT LEAST UNTIL DENDE REACHES THE EARTHLINGS...
THEY HOLD THE KEY TO THIS PLANET'S FATE NOW...

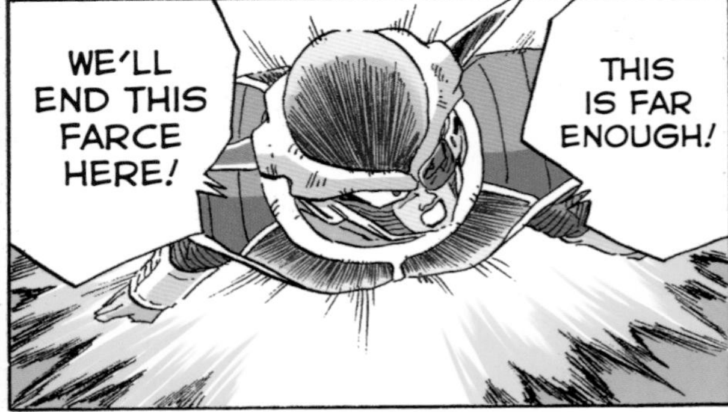

THIS IS FAR ENOUGH!
WE'LL END THIS FARCE HERE!

...

TOOM
TP

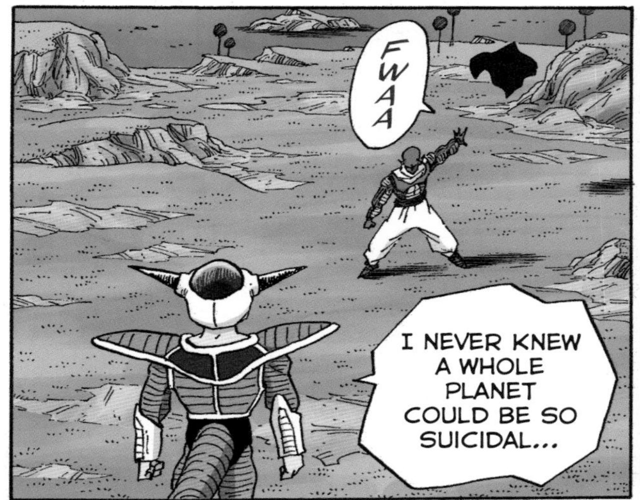
FWAA
I NEVER KNEW A WHOLE PLANET COULD BE SO SUICIDAL...

ザッ

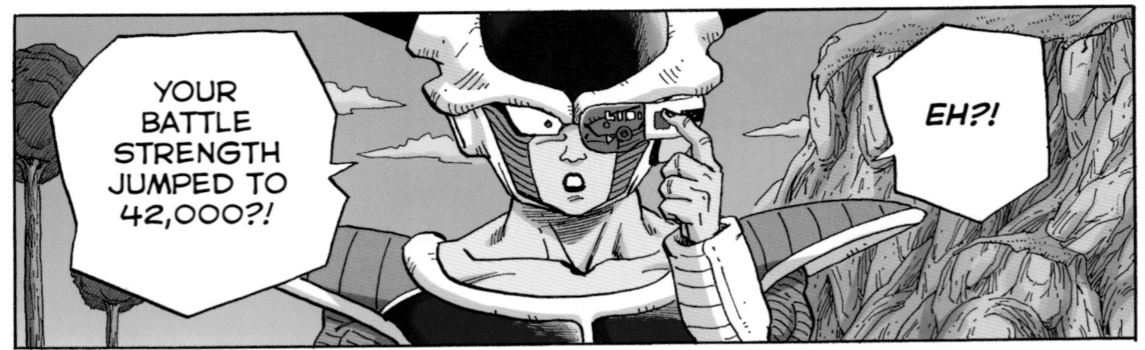
YOUR BATTLE STRENGTH JUMPED TO 42,000?!
EH?!

I SHOULD WARN YOU ABOUT MY OWN BATTLE STRENGTH, IN THE INTEREST OF FAIRNESS.

WELL THEN... YOU ***ARE*** DIFFERENT FROM THE OTHER NAMEKIANS!
APPARENTLY WHEN THEY CALL YOU A "WARRIOR" IT'S MORE THAN A JOB DESCRIPTION!
I ALMOST WANT YOU AS ONE OF MY MEN...

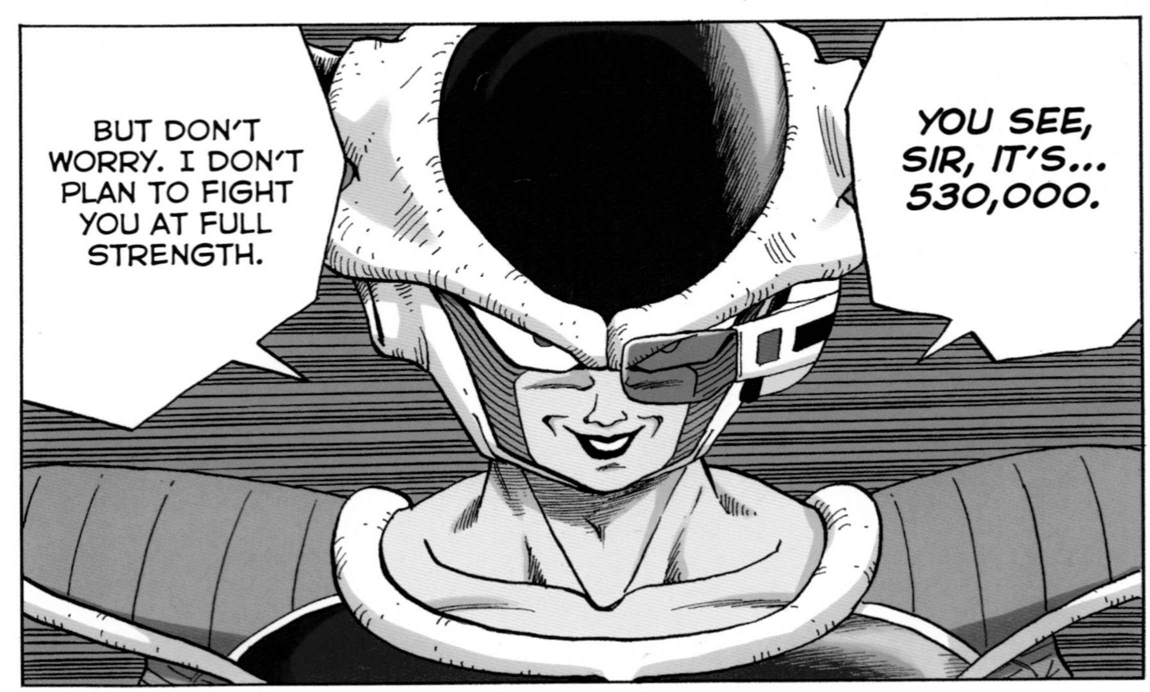
YOU SEE, SIR, IT'S... 530,000.
BUT DON'T WORRY. I DON'T PLAN TO FIGHT YOU AT FULL STRENGTH.

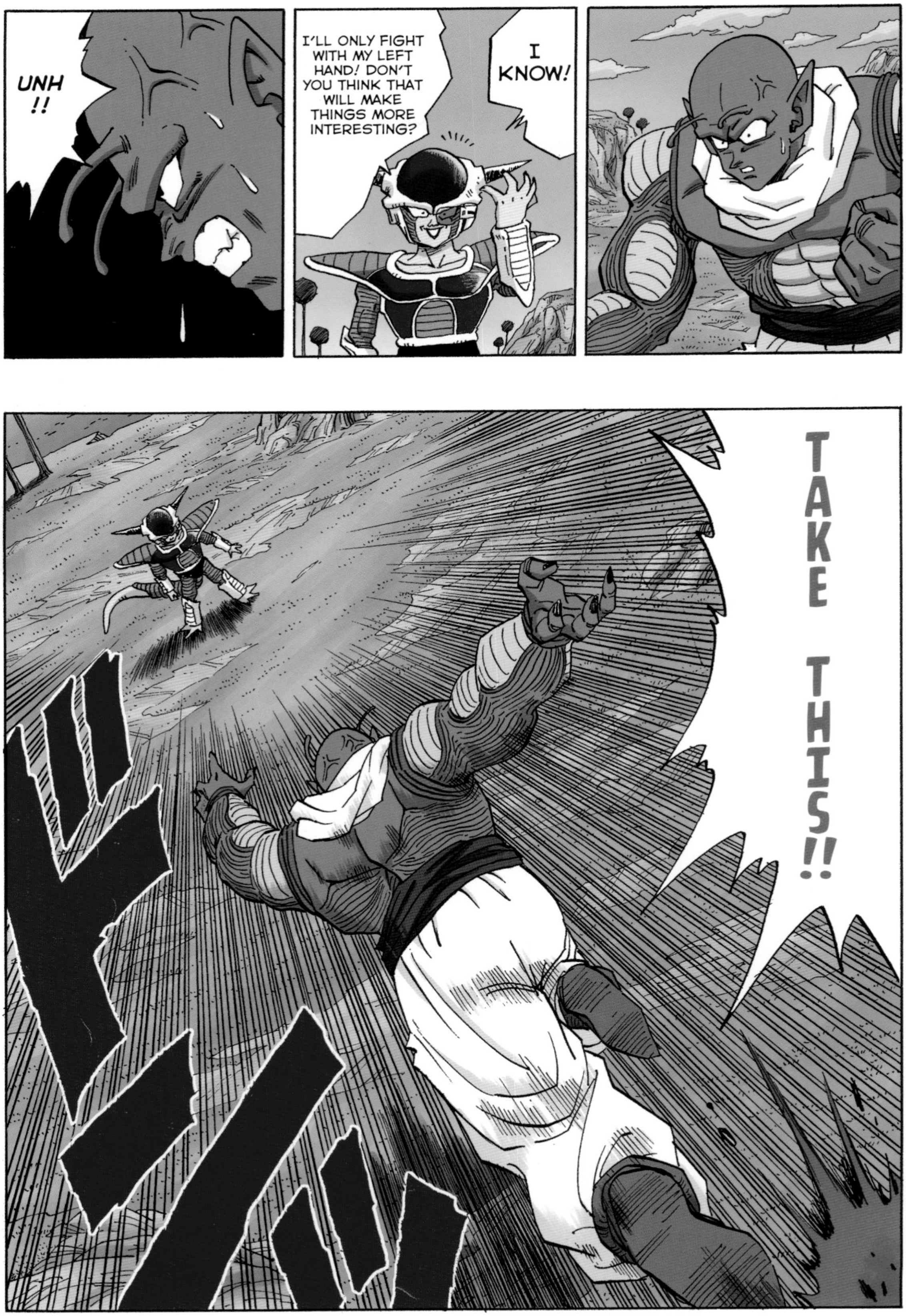

I KNOW!
I'LL ONLY FIGHT WITH MY LEFT HAND! DON'T YOU THINK THAT WILL MAKE THINGS MORE INTERESTING?

UNH!!

TAKE THIS!!

HYAH!!
NNNH...!!
I SUPPOSE THIS IS ALL I COULD EXPECT FROM 42,000...

ググッ...
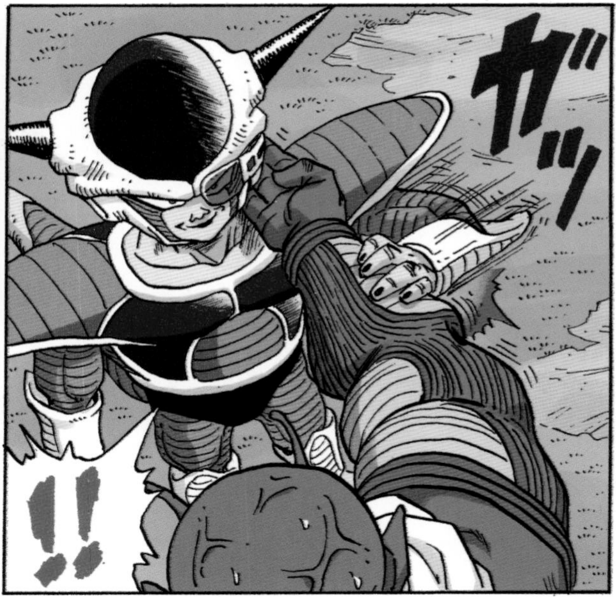
ガッ
!!

HNK...!!
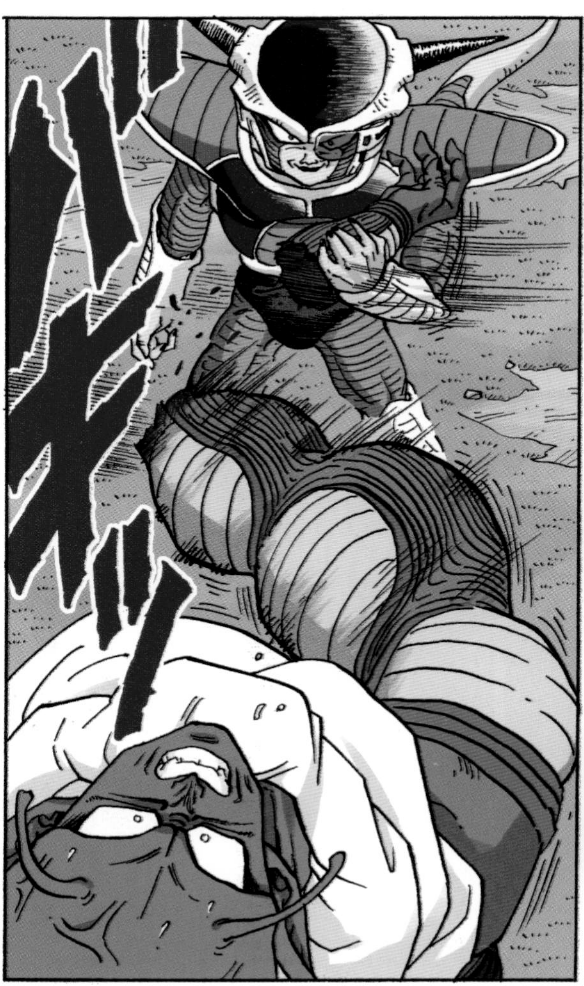
ゴッ

GUH...!!
AAAAA!!
GGK GGK

YAAAAH!!

UNH
...
UNH...
CAREFUL. DON'T PUSH YOURSELF.

JUST ANSWER MY QUESTION BEFORE YOU GET KILLED.
HUH *HUH*

OH, I AM SO SORRY.
NN... NNG ...!!

HYAAAAH!!

ズッ

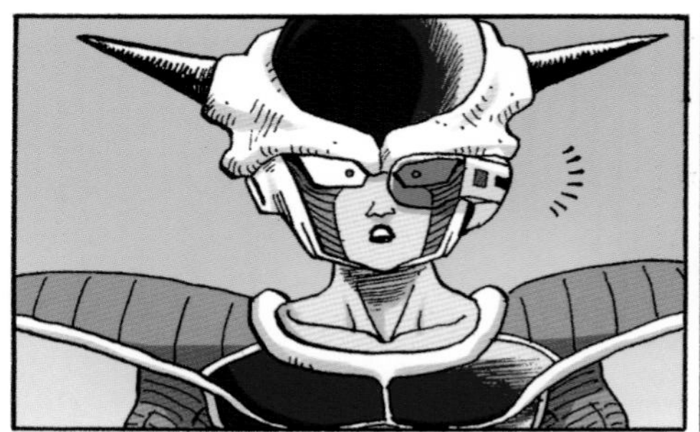

huff
huff
TWIK TWIK

MORE SURPRISES! YOU CAN RE-GENERATE?
AH, HOWEVER... YOUR ARM GROWS BACK, BUT YOUR BATTLE STRENGTH HAS GONE DOWN... AND STAYS THERE.

YOU DON'T MEAN YOU WANT TO KEEP FIGHTING EVEN AFTER THAT...?
FOR GOODNESS SAKE...I DON'T UNDERSTAND WHAT THE PEOPLE ON THIS PLANET ARE THINKING ...

WHAT'S SO FUNNY ...?!

YOU'RE SO STRONG ...
YOU HAVE POWERS FAR BEYOND MINE...

...?
YEAH...? SO WHY ARE YOU LAUGH-ING?!

!!
TH- THAT'S RIGHT! IT'S CAPTAIN GINYU!!

HEH HEH HEH ...
HA HA HA...!!

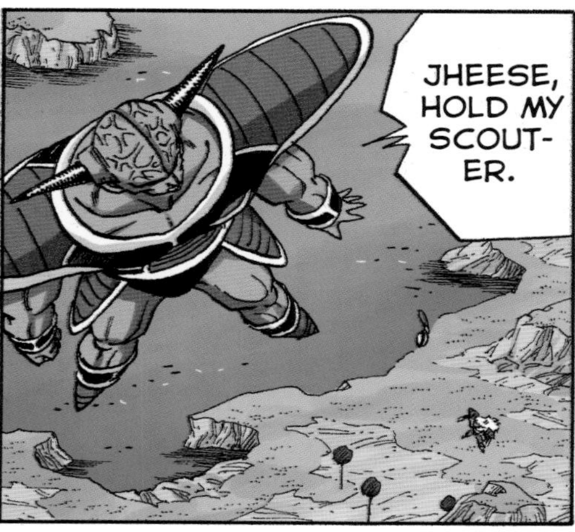
JHEESE, HOLD MY SCOUTER.

PFAP

THIS'LL BE GOOD!!

...?

HEH HEH HEH...

!!

GAH!!
W-WHAT ARE YOU ...?!!

SWITCH!!

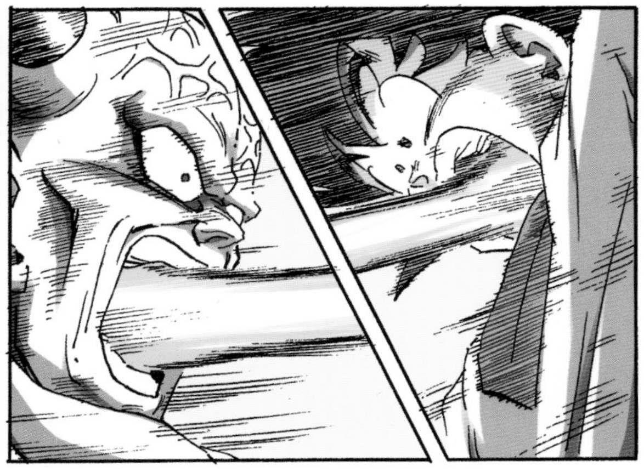

HEH
HEH
HEH
...
YEAH...I
LIKE IT A
LOT!!

AH...!!
AAA
...!!

Chapter 042 • The Switch

WE'RE HEADING BACK TO THE SPACESHIP! MASTER FREEZA MIGHT BE BACK BY NOW!
ALL RIGHT!

ARRRGH!! I...I CAN'T MOVE...!!
SO THIS IS WHY HE HURT HIMSELF...!

WHAT HAPPENS... WHEN THEY RUN INTO KURIRIN AND GOHAN...?!!
OHHH NO!!

OOOH, THIS BODY'S FAST!!
HA HA HA!!

UNH...
STOP...!!

EVEN IF I BEAT THE BAD GUYS...AND GET EVERYONE BACK TO EARTH SAFELY...
...WHAT'S MY WIFE GOING TO SAY?!

SHOOT...!! I'M NOT USED TO THIS BODY...AND WITH A WOUND ON TOP OF IT...I CAN'T EVEN FLY STRAIGHT!!
TH-THIS IS TERRIBLE!!

TP
TP
BULMA!!

ZZZ
ZZZ

B-BULMA!!
W-WHERE'S THE DRAGON RADAR?!!

MMM?

UMMM... W-WE NEED THE RADAR ...
WE STILL MIGHT BE ABLE TO GET OUR WISH GRANTED IF...

WHAT HAVE YOU BEEN DOING?! FIRST YOU CAME TO GET THE DRAGON BALL—WITH VEGETA IN TOW—THEN YOU TOOK OFF AGAIN!!
WHAT'S THE BIG IDEA OF LEAVING A GIRL ALL ALONE IN A PLACE LIKE THIS?!

WHAT?! YOU MEAN YOU STILL HAVEN'T GOTTEN IT GRANTED *YET?!*
I SAW ALL SEVEN DRAGON BALLS TOGETHER ON THE RADAR! I THOUGHT YOU'D CALLED SHENLONG AND WERE DONE WITH IT ALREADY! WHAT ARE YOU PLAYING AROUND FOR?!

PLAYING AROUND ...?!

I SEE IT, KURIRIN!! THAT WAY!!

ALL RIGHT!
LET'S GO!!

H-HEY, WHAT'S GOING ON HERE?!!
WE'RE IN KIND OF A HURRY NOW, SO...LATER!
OH, YEAH! DAD'S HERE!

GOHAN, LET'S GO!!

SON'S HERE?!
H-H-HOW DOES HE LOOK?! DID HE GET MORE POWERFUL?!

DID I BLOW IT...?
...

LITTLE SON GOKU...
WHO'D'VE THOUGHT HE'D BECOME THE ULTIMATE POWER...?
AND ME ALWAYS FIGHTING WITH YAMCHA, WHO'S SUPPOSED TO BE MY BOYFRIEND...

TP

HYUUU

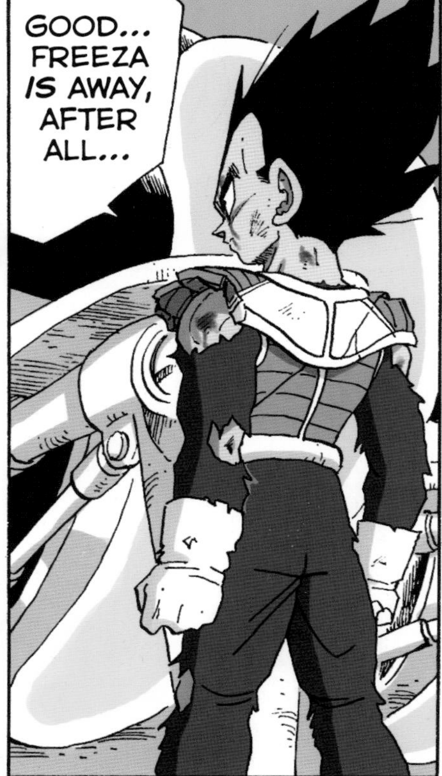
GOOD... FREEZA *IS* AWAY, AFTER ALL...

I DON'T SEE THE DRAGON BALLS...THEY MUST HAVE HIDDEN THEM... UNLESS FREEZA TOOK THEM...
THE WAY GINYU STAYED BEHIND, THEY MUST BE AROUND HERE... AND THOSE EARTHLINGS WILL BE LOOKING FOR THEM WITH THAT GADGET...

THEY'LL BE HERE SOON...
...PERHAPS I SHOULD CHANGE INTO FRESH BATTLE CLOTHES.

MY WOUNDS ARE HEALED...MY ENERGY'S BACK...
WHAT WAS THAT MEDICINE OF KAKARROT'S?

HMPH ...
THE ONLY ONE THAT FITS IS OUT OF STYLE...

EH?

HERE COME THE EARTH-LINGS.
I DON'T WANT THEM TO KNOW I'M HERE...I'LL HAVE TO SUPPRESS MY POWER LIKE THEY DO...

KURIRIN!! THERE...!!
Y-YEAH!! THAT MUST BE THEIR SPACESHIP!!

THE DRAGON BALL READINGS AREN'T IN THE SHIP... THEY'RE A LITTLE WAYS AWAY...
LET'S LOOK FOR 'EM, QUICK! NO-BODY'S AROUND!

TP
TP

WHERE ARE THEY, GOHAN?
UM... THIS WAY...
ALMOST THERE...

... WHAT...?

HERE! KURIRIN, THEY'RE HERE!!
OH YEAH! IT LOOKS LIKE A HOLE GOT DUG!! OK, LET'S DIG 'EM UP!

TP

THERE THEY ARE!!
IT LOOKS LIKE ALL SEVEN!!
SO THAT'S WHERE THEY WERE HIDDEN ...!

ALL RIGHT!! JUST SUMMON YOUR "SHENLONG" ...
THEN I'LL FINISH YOU TWO AND GET MY WISH—ETERNAL LIFE!!

HA HA HA!!
WE GOT 'EM ALL!!

ALLLLRIGHTY! HERE GOES! THE MOMENT WE'VE BEEN WAITING FOR!
THE SUMMONING OF SHENLONG!!
AND BRINGING EVERYBODY BACK TO LIFE!!

WELL?!! WHY DON'T YOU DO IT?!!

WE SURE WENT THROUGH A LOT, DIDN'T WE...?
YEAH...

ANYWAY...
DRAGON, COME FORTH!! GRANT ME THIS WISH!!

THAT'S THE SECRET INVOCATION ...?!

...
...

WHAT...?! WASN'T SOMETHING SUPPOSED TO HAPPEN?!
WHAT IS SHENLONG?!

I-IT SHOULD BE HERE BY NOW... SHOULDN'T IT...?
B-BUT WHY...?!

WHY DIDN'T SHENLONG COME BURSTING OUT?!
MAYBE THE WORDS ARE DIFFERENT HERE!!
WHAT ARE THOSE PUNKS DOING...?!

EH?!

K-KURIRIN!
S-SOME-ONE'S COMING THIS WAY!
WHAT?!

H-HEY, I FEEL TWO CHI!!
I-IS THAT GINYU AND THE OTHER JERK?!
THEN WHAT HAPPENED TO DAD?! DID HE GET KILLED?!

BLAST IT...!
THIS IS GETTING MORE AND MORE ANNOYING!!

SUP-PRESS YOUR *CHI* AND HIDE, GOHAN!!

B-BUT WHAT HAP-PENED TO GOKU?!
THEY'RE EVIL!! THERE'S NO DOUBT ABOUT IT!! IT'S THEM!!

HUH ?!
?!

スタッ
スタッ

DRAGON BALL FULL COLOR FREEZA ARC

HUH?!

HEY!

Chapter 043 • Goku or Ginyu?!

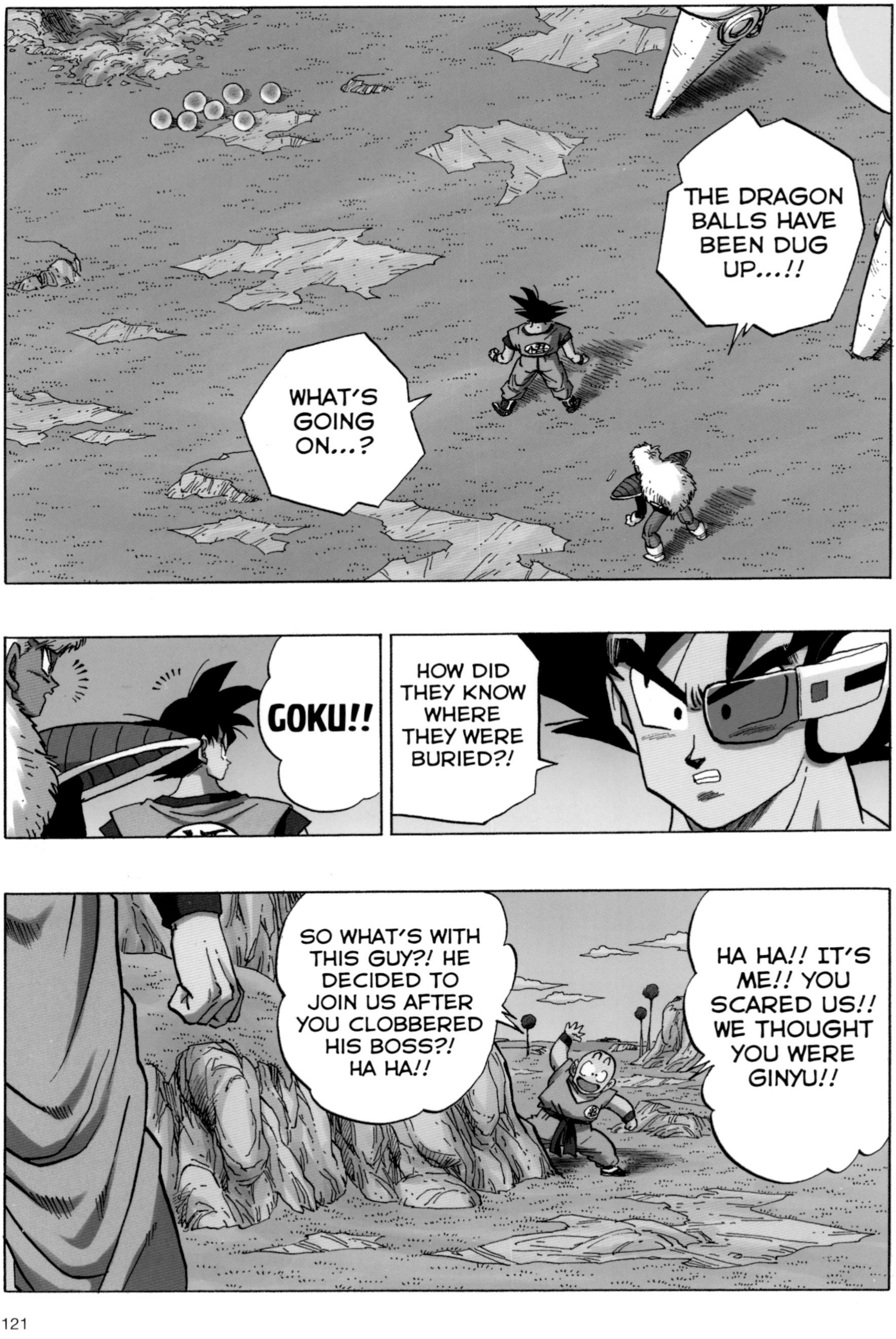

THE DRAGON BALLS HAVE BEEN DUG UP...!!

WHAT'S GOING ON...?

WHAT ARE YOU TALKIN' ABOUT?! WITH THE DRAGON RADAR, OF COURSE!
WERE YOU THE ONE WHO FOUND THE DRAGON BALLS...? HOW DID YOU KNOW...?

WE DON'T KNOW WHY... UNLESS MAYBE THE INVOCATION'S DIFFERENT FROM ON EARTH...

WE DIDN'T EVEN GET SHENLONG! HE NEVER CAME OUT!
HECK...

"RADAR"... CHEATERS...
AND DID YOU GET YOUR WISH?

THEN YOU DIDN'T...
I SEE...

...

...GOKU, IS THERE SOMETHING WRONG...?
I MEAN... YOU SEEM DIFFERENT... AND WHY DO YOU HAVE ONE O' THEIR *SCOUTERS* ON...?

YOU REALLY WANT TO KNOW?
HUH?

KURIRIN!!
THAT'S NOT DAD!!

WHAT?!

バキッ

NNH!!

!!

SO THERE WAS ANOTHER ONE OF THEM...
THERE WAS NO READING ON THE SCOUTER. HE MUST BE ABLE TO SUPPRESS HIS BATTLE STRENGTH DOWN TO ZERO...

... WHAT...?!
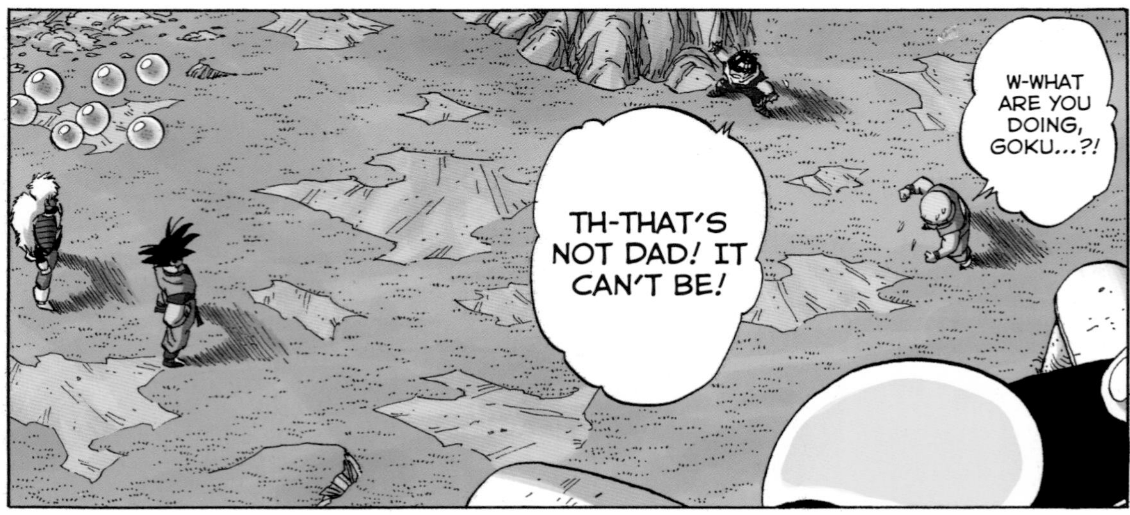
W-WHAT ARE YOU DOING, GOKU...?!
TH-THAT'S NOT DAD! IT CAN'T BE!

N-NOT GOKU...? B-B-BUT HE LOOKS JUST...
I KNOW! BUT I CAN TELL!

WE SWITCHED BODIES.
THIS ONE WAS SO MUCH MORE POWERFUL.

MY NAME IS GINYU...
LEADER OF THE GINYU SPECIAL FORCE!!

!!

S-SAY WHAT...?!

SWITCHED ...?!

THIS IS A PERFECT TIME TO TEST IT...

HOW... HOW... HOW... HOW...?!

シュー・・・ッ

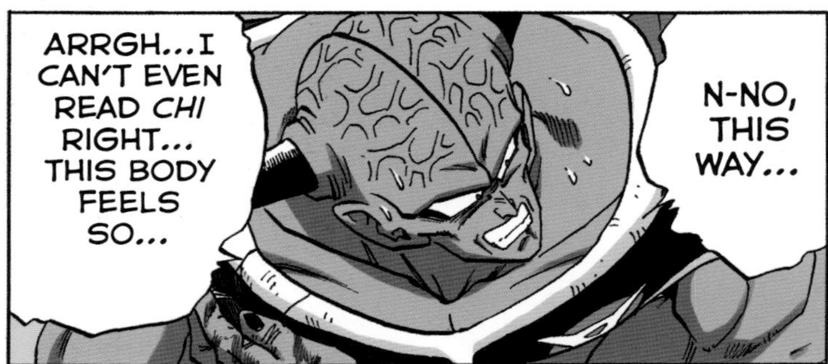
ARRGH...I CAN'T EVEN READ *CHI* RIGHT... THIS BODY FEELS SO...
N-NO, THIS WAY...

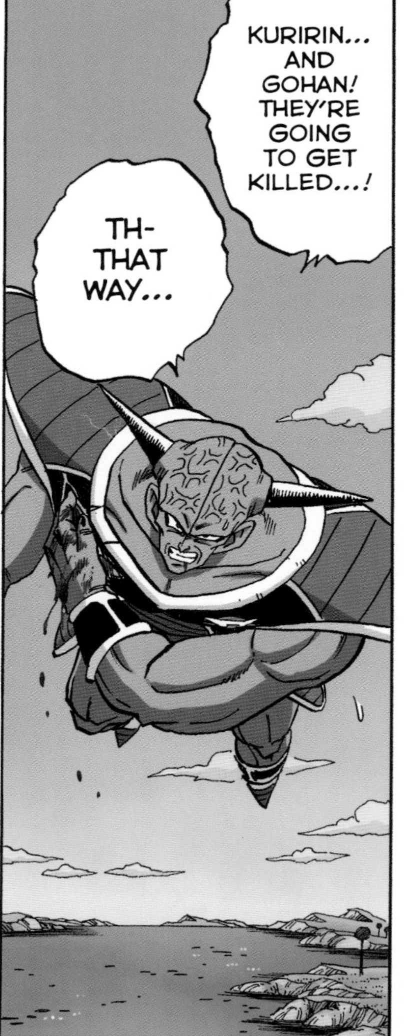
KURIRIN... AND GOHAN! THEY'RE GOING TO GET KILLED...!
TH-THAT WAY...

TH-THAT'S IT!!

...!
...SO WEIRD!!

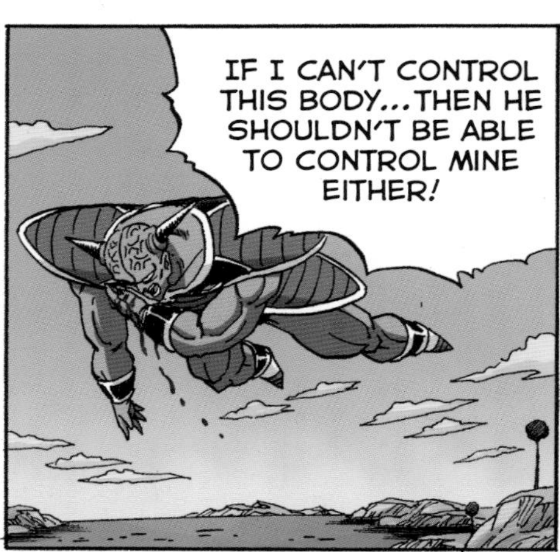
IF I CAN'T CONTROL THIS BODY...THEN HE SHOULDN'T BE ABLE TO CONTROL MINE EITHER!

HA HA
HA!!

C'MON
C'MON!!

THIS IS GETTING EVEN MORE ANNOYING...
WHETHER THEY SWITCHED BODIES OR HE'S UNDER HYPNOSIS, IT'S STILL KAKARROT'S POWER...

HA HA HA!!
I'M GOING TO INCREASE MY POWER BIT BY BIT!! ARE YOU READY?!
ビシッ
ビビッ
Pi Piii
HUH?

ACK!

CAPTAIN GINYU!
HE'S COME AFTER US!

WHAT?

I...I FOUND THEM...!

AMAZING THAT YOU MADE IT THIS FAR...*HEH HEH HEH*...I SHOULD'VE WOUNDED MYSELF MORE DEEPLY!

TP

OH... GEEZ ...
TH-TH-THEN... IT'S TRUE ...?!

Y-YOU MEAN ...
... THAT'S DAD ...?!

KURIRIN, GOHAN... L-LISTEN...!! THAT'S NOT ME! HE SWITCHED BODIES!!

HE'S GINYU!! DON'T HOLD BACK!! FIGHT HIM!!
TOGETHER YOU CAN'T LOSE!! JUST WHALE ON HIM!

EASY TO SAY... BUT...
HA HA HA! FOOL! THEY CAN'T LOSE, YOU SAY?!
IT'S YOUR BODY! ITS BATTLE STRENGTH IS OVER 180,000!! THERE'S NO WAY THEY CAN WIN!!

YOU GOT ONE THING RIGHT!
THAT'S MY BODY!! YOU CAN'T CONTROL THE CHI!! YOU COULD NEVER PULL OFF A KAIÓ-KEN!!
I BET YOU WON'T EVEN BE ABLE TO BRING OUT HALF MY POWER!!

HEH HEH HEH... YOU THINK BLUFFS WILL FOOL ME...?
TAKE A LOOK AT THIS!!

NRRAUGH!!!

HA HA HA...!!
JHEESE!! WHAT'S MY BATTLE STRENGTH?!

... IT'S...
...UM... 23,000...

...JUST 23,000...?!

NGH!!

IT'S IMPOSSIBLE ...!!
HOW C-COULD IT BE...?!

GOKU WAS RIGHT ...!!
WE CAN WIN THIS...!!

JHEESE!! WHY ARE YOU STANDING THERE?! FIGHT!!
OH! Y-YESSIR !!

NOT SO FAST!
YOU'RE GOING TO FIGHT ME!

VEGETA ...!

Chapter 044 • Ginyu's Mistake!

HYAH!!
YAAAH!!
YOU THOUGHT *THAT* PIDDLY ATTACK WOULD HURT ME?!!

W-WHAT IS THIS...?!
THIS BODY SHOULD BE ABLE TO PRODUCE A POWER OVER 180,000...!!

LIKE GOKU SAID, STUPID—YOU DON'T KNOW HOW TO USE THAT BODY!
YOU SHOULD GIVE UP WHILE YOU CAN!

GIVE UP...?
GINYU... GIVE UP?!

YOU DON'T KNOW GINYU!!

DAH!!

VEGETA?!! H-HOW DID YOU HIDE?!! THERE WAS NO READING ON THE SCOUTER!!
YOU FOOLS DEPEND ON THOSE SCOUTERS TOO MUCH!
YOU'LL LEARN THAT BY THE TIME YOU'VE FINISHED THIS FIGHT!

OF COURSE... BY THAT TIME YOU'LL BE DEAD...

SHUT UP!! YOU'RE NO MATCH FOR ME!!
バギッ

HEH... YOU DO KNOW, DON'T YOU...
...HOW STRONG I'VE BECOME?
TAKE A GOOD LOOK WITH YOUR PRECIOUS SCOUTER...

SO WHAT?!
YOU THINK *JHEESE* IS AFRAID OF *YOUR* POWER?!

PII PII PII

...
N-NO...

IMPOSSIBLE!!
IT'S BROKEN!!
KRAK
HEH HEH HEH... DO YOU REALLY BELIEVE THAT?

IT'S TRUE, YOU KNOW...I'VE SURPASSED THE LIMITS OF THE SAIYAN RACE...AND I'M STILL GETTING STRONGER.
AND I'M JUST BEGINNING TO REALIZE THAT THIS IS MORE THAN AN ORDINARY INCREASE.

HEH... KAKARROT WON'T BE ABLE TO DO IT...HE'S TOO SOFT-HEARTED. BUT I'M DIFFERENT!
W-WHAT ?!
SHYEAH RIGHT!

IN OTHER WORDS ...
...I'M GETTING CLOSER AND CLOSER...
...TO BECOMING A *SUPER SAIYAN!*

HAH!!

ベキッ

!!

HEH ...

GAG!!

!!

!!
!!

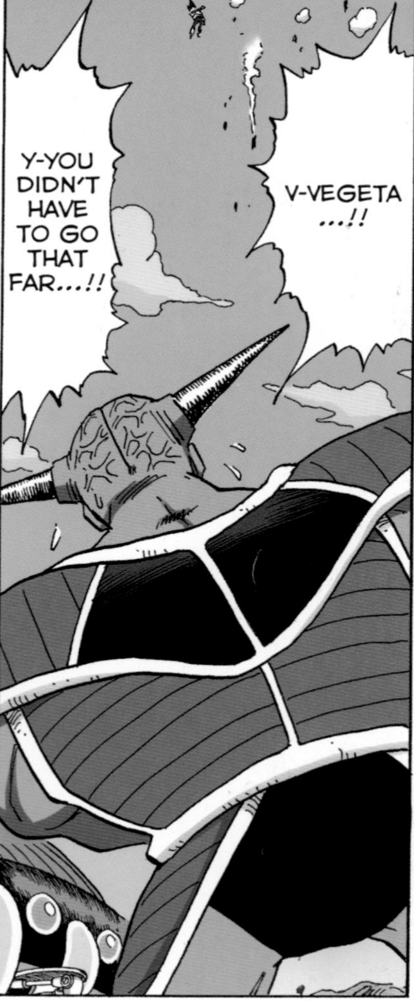
V-VEGETA ...!!
Y-YOU DIDN'T HAVE TO GO THAT FAR...!!

THAT'S IT... JUST KEEP ON BEING SOFT, KAKARROT...
LEAVE THAT SUPER SAIYAN STATUS TO ME.

V-VEGETA... KILLED JHEESE...?!!
THIS... THIS CAN'T BE...!!

TSK. HAVEN'T YOU FOOLS DONE AWAY WITH GINYU YET?
IT'S BECAUSE HE LOOKS LIKE KAKARROT, ISN'T IT?!
FINE! I'LL TAKE CARE OF HIM!

OUT OF THE WAY!!
!!

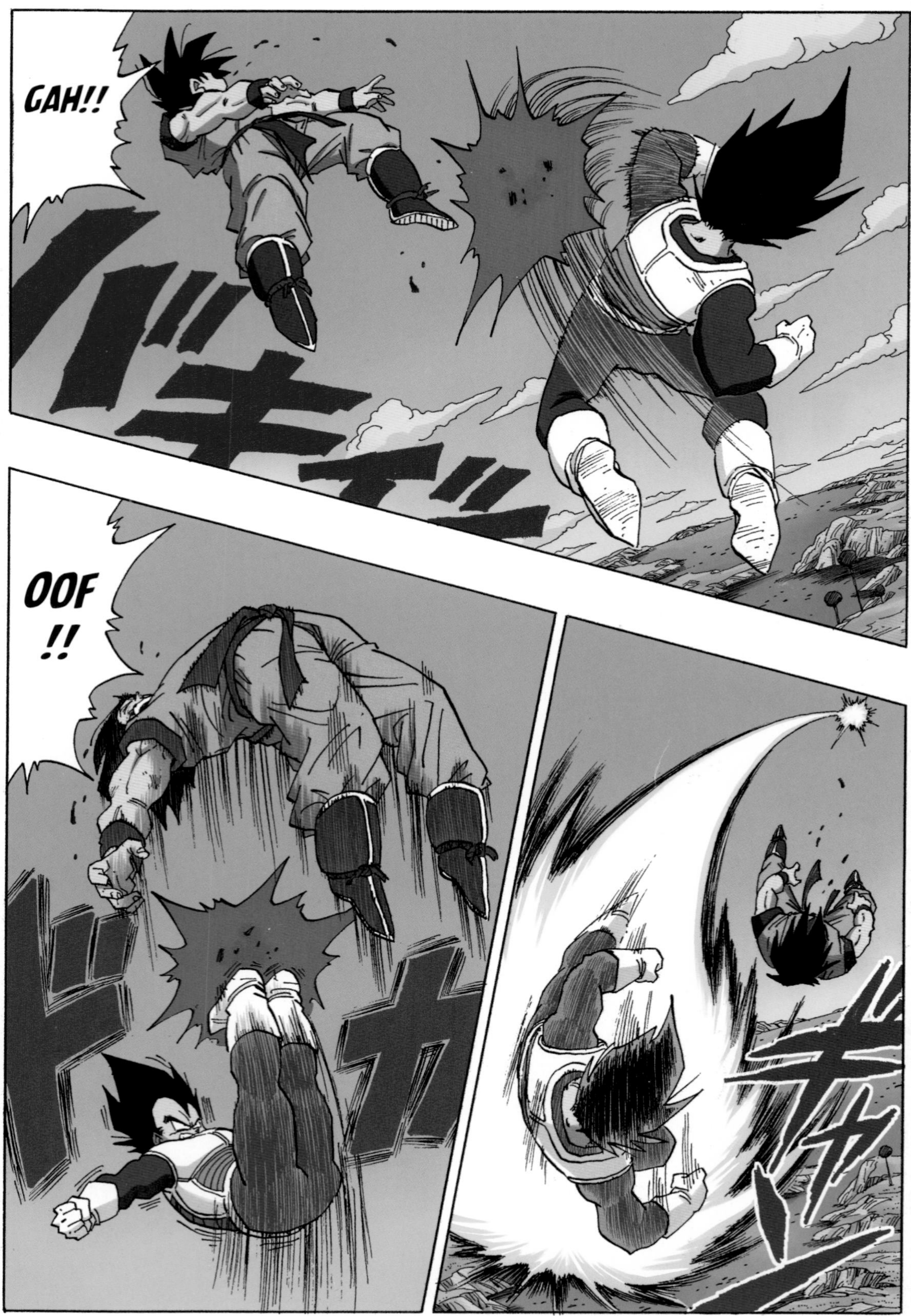
GAH!!
OOF !!

RAAAH!!

AHH...
UNH...

WATCH ME!!

C...CURSE YOU...

W-WHOA...
W-WOW...

TH-THAT'S ENOUGH, VEGETA!! DON'T KILL HIM!!

DIE!!!

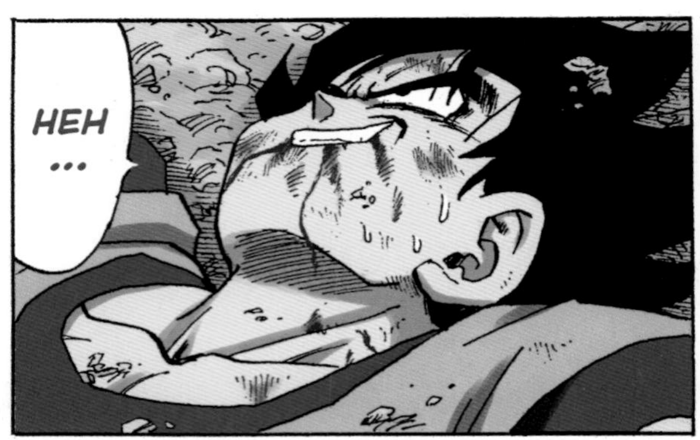
HEH
...

YES!!
HE...
HE IS
...!!

NOW
!!!

THIS IS MY CHANCE !!
I CAN GET BACK TO MY OWN BODY!!

バンッ

PLEASE, MAKE IT IN TIME!!
バッ

WHAT ?!!

EH-?!!
N-NO-!!!

NKH!!
タッ

UHH...F... FOOL...!!
HE GOT... IN THE WAY...!!

HEH... HEH HEH... OUCH...
I GUESS I'M... BACK...!

WHAT DID HE DO JUST NOW...?
W-WHAT ...?!

DAD'S BACK IN HIS REAL BODY!!
I CAN FEEL IT–IT'S DAD!!

OH!!

W-WHAT WAS THAT LIGHT...?
D-DID GOKU GO TO STOP VEGETA'S ATTACK...?

AARGH!! THIS TIME I'LL GET VEGETA!!

ARE YOU SURE, GOHAN ?!
WHAT?!

UH-OH...I CAN'T MOVE WITH ALL THESE INJURIES...!
I-IT'S ALL OVER IF HE GETS VEGETA'S BODY NOW...

GEH HEH HEH...THAT WAS POOR PLANNING ON YOUR PART... YOU CAN'T INTERFERE ANYMORE!

HA HA HA ...!!
I'M TAKING THAT BODY!!

THEN ...
IS THAT GINYU NOW...?!

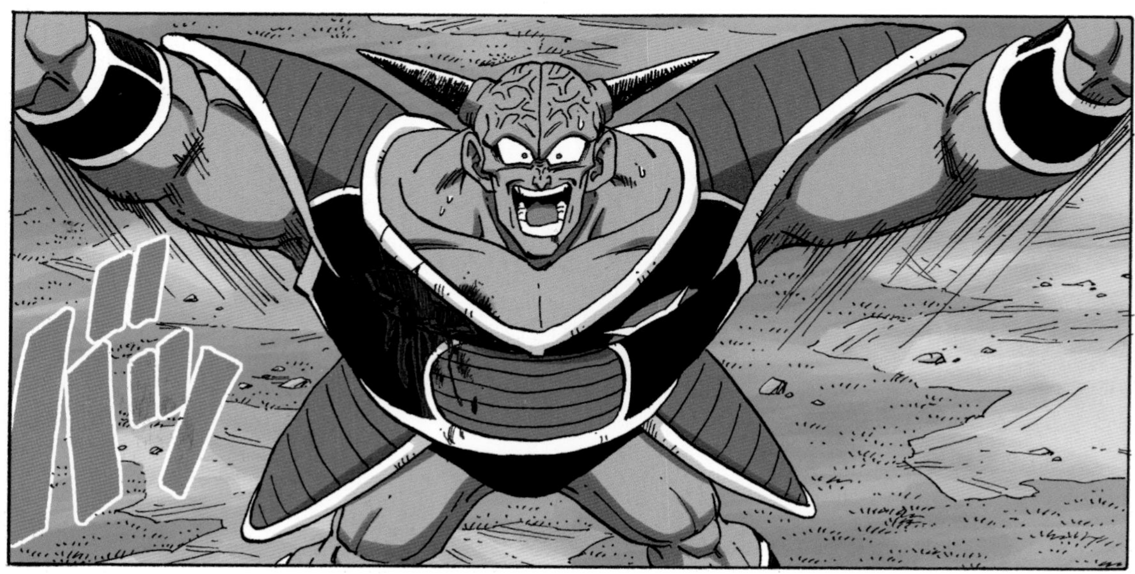
バッ

!!

SWITCH!!!

GGH!
ribbit

...
N-NOW WHAT...?!

ペタン

BOING
BOING

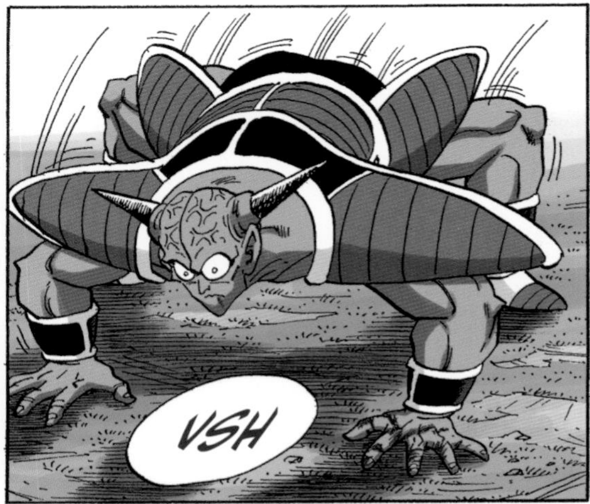
VSH

I...I DID IT...
HA...HA HA...

...?
...

TMP
TMP
TMP

G-GOKU? ARE YOU OK?!
DAD, HANG ON!!

YOU...REALLY BEAT UP MY BODY, DIDN'T YOU, VEGETA...?
WHAT HAPPENED TO GINYU?

HEH HEH HEH... THE ONE THAT RAN AWAY IS A FROG...
AND THAT FROG-LIKE THING OVER THERE...IS GINYU.

WHAT ?!

ribbit
ribbit
!!

I DON'T UNDERSTAND THIS, BUT...
I'M NOT LEAVING IT ALIVE!

ribbit ribbit

DROP IT, VEGETA.
HE CAN'T DO ANYTHING NOW.

HMPH.
ALL RIGHT, THEN. I'LL LET YOU OFF. THE LIFE YOU HAVE AHEAD OF YOU IS TORTURE ENOUGH.

SAY GOKU, DON'T YOU HAVE ANY MORE SENZU?
N-NO ...

HEH HEH HEH...
IT WOULD BE EASY TO BLOW YOU PESTS AWAY RIGHT NOW.

THERE'S THE MATTER OF THE DRAGON BALLS...AND THE FACT THAT I'LL NEED SOME HELP FIGHTING FREEZA...
HEH HEH HEH... YOU'RE RIGHT.

VEGETA... YOU LOUSY...
I-IT'S OKAY. H-HE CAN'T KILL US NOW...

...
MOVE IT! WE DON'T KNOW WHEN FREEZA'S COMING BACK!

WE'LL HAVE TO TREAT KAKARROT'S WOUNDS AND GET HIM UP TO FULL POWER.
BRING HIM INSIDE THE SPACE-SHIP...

BLUB
BLUB

I'LL DEAL WITH YOU AT MY LEISURE ONCE FREEZA'S FINISHED!
BY THEN, AFTER ALL, I'LL BE A SUPER SAIYAN!

PITY I DESTROYED THE NEWER MODELS.
THE MEDICAL MACHINES IN THIS ROOM ARE OLDER, BUT THEY SHOULD BE ADEQUATE.
H-HE WON'T DROWN, WILL HE...?
I'LL HAVE TO GET YOU TWO SOME BATTLE CLOTHES. THEY'LL PROVIDE SOME PROTECTION.
NOW THEN.
HUH? BATTLE CLOTHES... YOU MEAN LIKE ***YOURS?***
THAT'S GONNA FEEL WEIRD...
BLUB BLUB
H-HEY... THIS FEELS GOOD...

FWAP

TAKE YOUR CLOTHES OFF AND PUT ON THOSE UNDER-SUITS.
MAKE IT QUICK! FREEZA'S COMING!

THIS TECHNOLOGY IS WAY BEYOND OURS...
NO KIDDING...

NOW FOR THE BATTLE JACKETS.
LUCKILY THERE WERE SOME MINIATURE ONES...MADE FOR THE PEOPLE OF THE PLANET LILLIPUT.

IF *VEGETA* NEEDS *OUR* HELP...THIS FREEZA MUST BE REALLY SOME-THING...
I'M KINDA SCARED...
tong

FORCE IT ON! THEY'LL STRETCH ENOUGH IF YOU PULL ON THEM.
THEY DIDN'T RIP WHEN I BECAME A GREAT APE ON EARTH, DID THEY?
AND THEY'LL WITHSTAND MOST IMPACTS.

...? HOW DO YOU PUT THIS ON?
MY HEAD FITS BUT MY SHOUL-DERS WON'T...

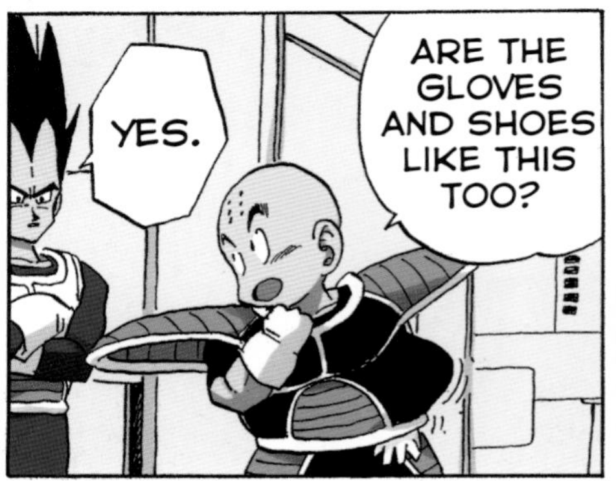
ARE THE GLOVES AND SHOES LIKE THIS TOO?
YES.

OH!!
WOW! YOU'RE RIGHT!

THIS ONE'S IN THE OLDER STYLE. I COULDN'T FIND A STANDARD SET THAT FIT ME.
BUT I'D RATHER HAVE ONE LIKE YOURS...IT LOOKS EASIER TO MOVE THE SHOULDERS.
BUT THEY DON'T GET IN THE WAY AT ALL, KURIRIN! I CAN MOVE MY ARMS EASY!
IT'S NOT FAIR! YOU GUYS HAVE ALL THE COOL STUFF!
IT'S SO LIGHT! I DON'T FEEL IT AT ALL!

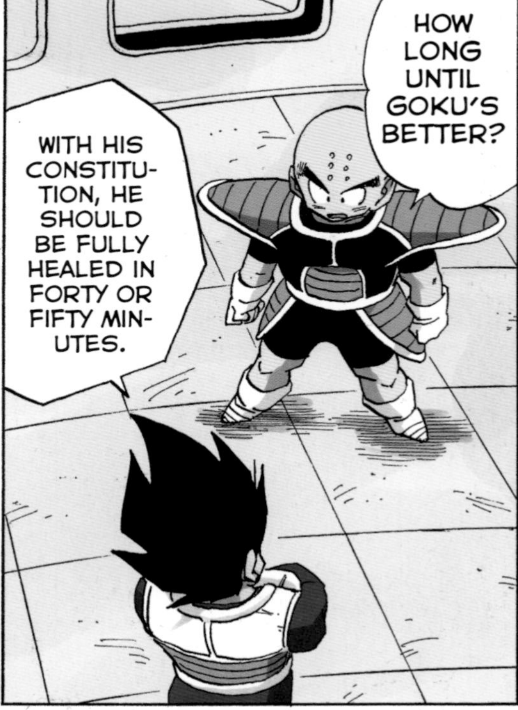

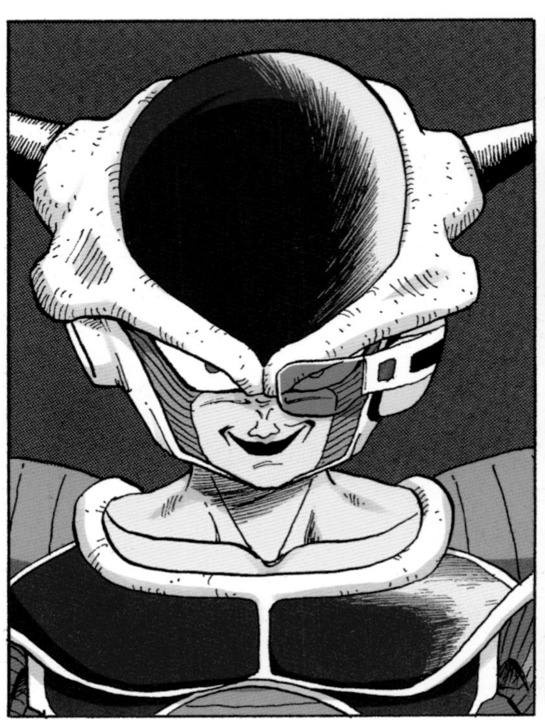

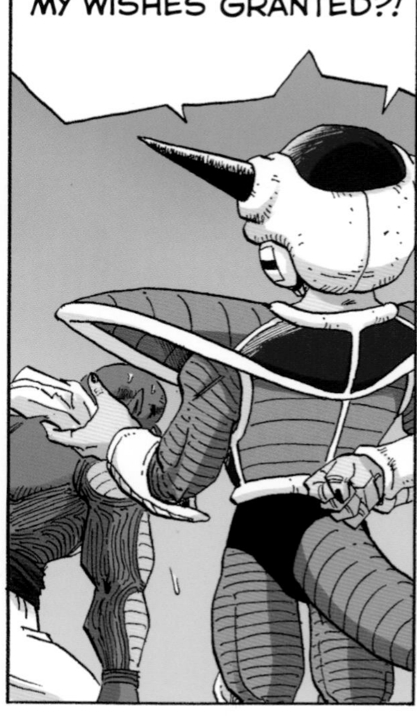
WHY WON'T YOU JUST TELL ME? I'M ONLY USING ONE ARM—AND STILL YOU'RE HELPLESS! WHAT DO I DO WITH THE DRAGON BALLS?! HOW DO I GET MY WISHES GRANTED?!

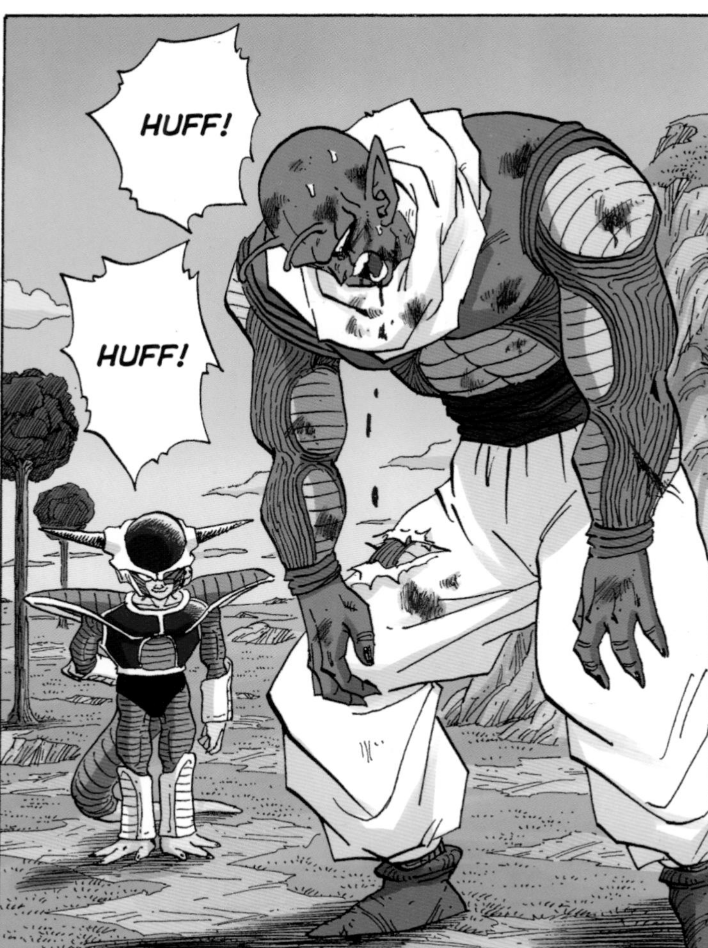
HUFF!
HUFF!

HAH!!

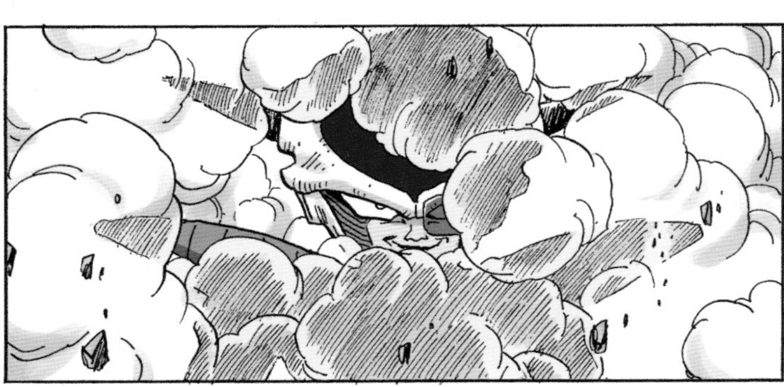

!!

YOUR STRUG-GLES ARE A WASTE.
SUCH AN ATTACK WILL NEVER WORK AGAINST ME.

WHY DO YOU FIGHT ON WHEN YOU MUST KNOW THAT YOU ARE GOING TO LOSE?
BECAUSE YOUR FRIENDS WERE KILLED? OR JUST BECAUSE YOU ARE STUBBORN?

ビッ

パッ
!!

バキッ

THIS WILL BE MY LAST WARNING.
NN... NNH... GAH...!!
TELL ME THE INCANTATION OR YOU WILL DIE!

HEH... HEH HEH...
I-IT'S TOO LATE. EVEN IF I TELL YOU NOW...

TOO LATE...?!

BY NOW... DENDE WILL HAVE REACHED THE EARTH-LINGS...
...AND TOLD THEM WHAT YOU WANT TO KNOW SO MUCH...

W-
WHAT ?!!

I-IT MUST HAVE BEEN HIM...!!

BLAST YOU!!
SO YOU WERE ONLY BUYING TIME!!

THE READINGS OF THE GINYU SPECIAL FORCE ARE GONE...!! IMPOSSIBLE... ALL FIVE OF THEM...!!
THEY COULDN'T BE DEAD ...?!!
SOMETHING'S HAPPENED, IN ANY CASE... BETWEEN VEGETA, THE EARTHLINGS AND THE GINYU SPECIAL FORCE!! AND THE DRAGON BALLS WERE...
CURSE THEM!!!

I DESERVE THIS POWER!!!
NOT YOU LOWER LIFE-FORMS!!

A-A LITTLE FARTHER ...!!
THE GREAT ELDER SAID THEY'RE IN THE SHELL REGION...!

I NEVER IMAGINED IT WOULD COME TO THIS...I SHOULD HAVE TOLD THE EARTHLING THE INCANTATION WHEN HE WAS HERE...

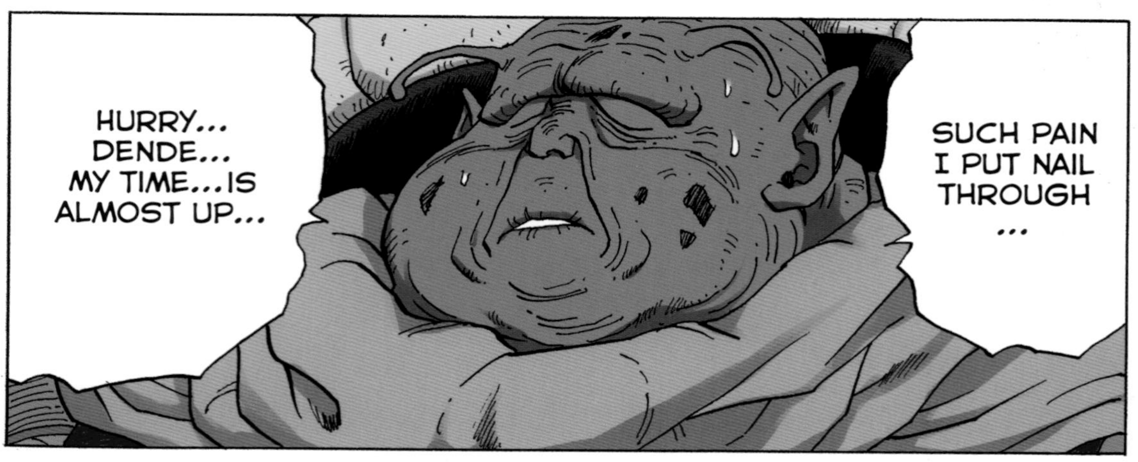
SUCH PAIN I PUT NAIL THROUGH ...
HURRY... DENDE... MY TIME...IS ALMOST UP...

!!
S-SOME-THING'S FLYING!!
...THAT *CHI*... IT'S...!!

... DENDE!!
HEH !!

HUH ?!
EEK !!!

HA HA!!
DON'T MIND THE CLOTHES, IT'S ME!!
KURIRIN !!!

YAH !!

Chapter 047 • The True Dragon God

I GUESS IT WOULD TAKE A COUPLE HOURS FOR KURIRIN TO GET TO THE GREAT ELDER'S AND BACK...
WHAT SHOULD I DO IF FREEZA COMES BACK...?

Z Z
Z Z

HUH?

S-SOME-ONE'S COMING!
IT'S NOT FREEZA! KURIRIN...?! BUT I FEEL TWO *CHI*...

OH! THEY SUPPRESSED THEIR *CHI*!!

IT IS KURIRIN!!
THE OTHER ONE IS... DENDE!! *YAY!!*

WE'RE IN LUCK, GOHAN!

THAT WAS REALLY FAST!! HOW'D YOU DO THAT?!
DENDE WAS ON THE WAY HERE!

TO TELL US HOW TO GRANT OUR WISH?!
YES!!

BUT WHERE'S VEGETA? WE SURPRESSED OUR *CHI* SO HE WOULDN'T SPOT US.
I THINK HE'S STILL ASLEEP...
HE SAID HE HADN'T SLEPT FOR A WHILE...

OKAY!! LISTEN—THIS IS THE BREAK WE NEED!! WE GOTTA GET ALL SEVEN DRAGON BALLS OUTTA HERE WITHOUT VEGETA NOTICING!!
HE CAN'T KNOW WHAT'S HAPPENING UNTIL AFTER SHENLONG COMES OUT...GOT THAT?

ZMM
ZMM

こそこそ・・・・・

PHEW!

EEE-HAW! WE DID IT!!

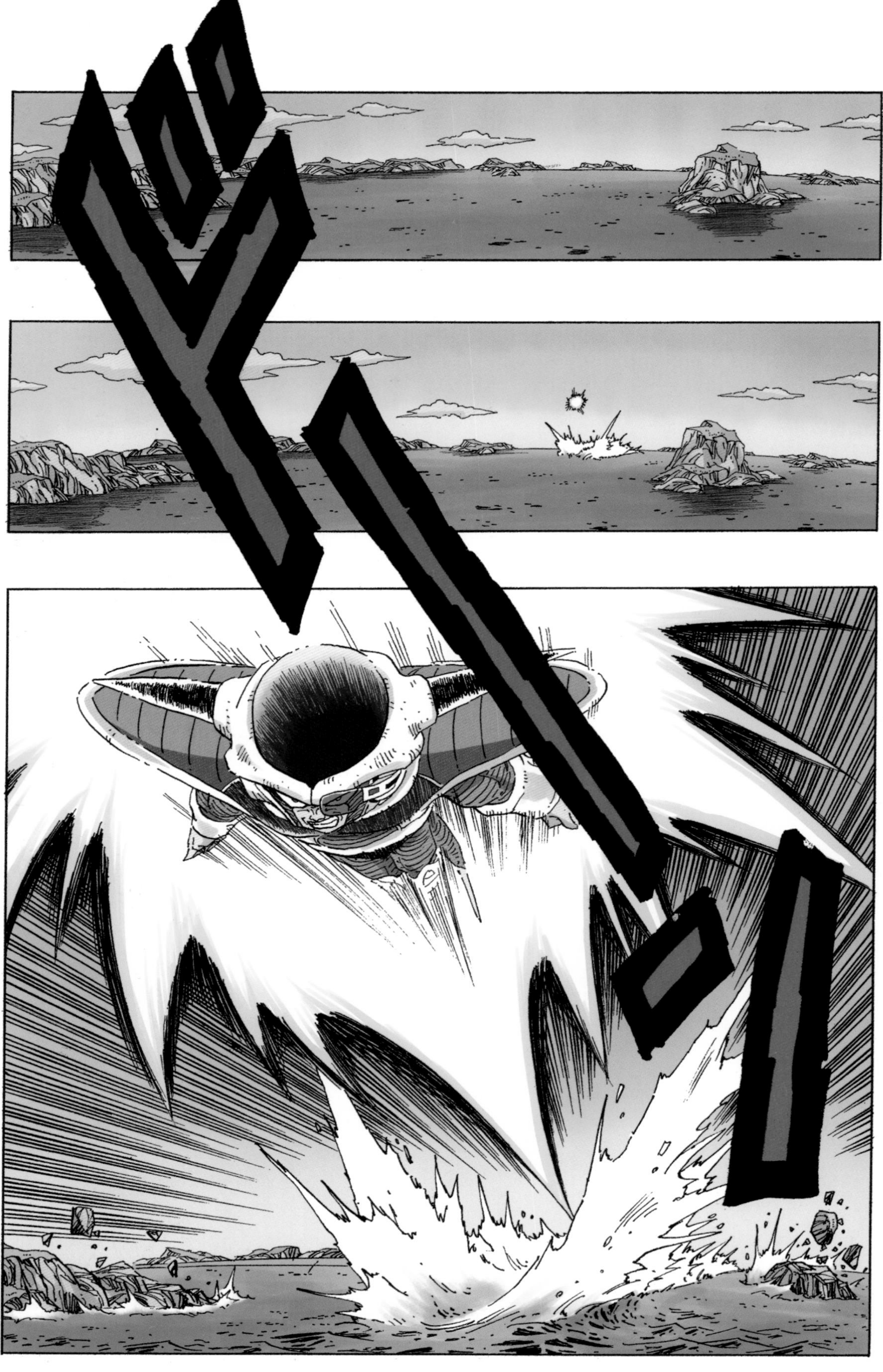

DENDE, HURRY!!
GET OUR WISH GRANTED!!
Y-Y-YES!!

TAKKARAPTO
POPPORUNGA
PUPIRITTO PARO

THEY'RE G-GLOWING...!!
ボ

OH!!
TH-THE SKY TURNED DARK!!
JUST LIKE WITH THE DRAGON BALLS ON EARTH!
WAAGH !!

WHAT'S HAPPENING?!

WHY IS IT *DARK...?!*

HOO-HOO!! THE DRAGON GOD IS COMING!!

YES!!

ゴゴゴゴーー

I SHALL GRANT ANY THREE WISHES WITHIN MY POWER.

O MASTER OF THE DRAGON BALLS, STATE YOUR WISH.

F-FIRST... PLEASE BRING THE PEOPLE WHO WERE KILLED BY THE SAIYANS ON EARTH BACK TO LIFE!!

ONLY ONE BEING AT A TIME CAN BE RESTORED TO LIFE.
THAT I CANNOT DO.

HMM... IT SEEMS THAT ONLY ONE OF YOU CAN BE RESTORED PER WISH...

WHAT?!
OHHH... NO...!!

ONLY *ONE?!*

PLEASE!!
LET ME TALK TO GOHAN!!

STATE YOUR WISHES, I SHALL GRANT ANY THREE WITHIN MY POWER.

SPEAK!

Chapter 048 • The Three Wishes

JUST LET ME TALK TO HIM!!
YOU WANT TO SPEAK TO SON GOKU'S SON?! WHAT ARE YOU UP TO...?!

GOHAN!! CAN YOU HEAR ME?! IT'S PICCOLO.

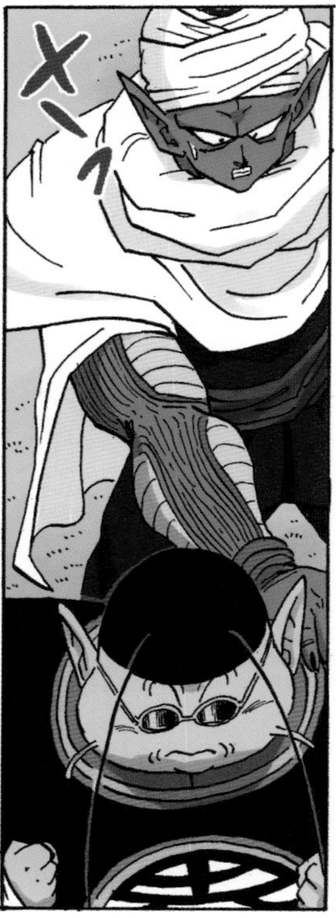

WELL...ALL RIGHT...! P-PUT YOUR HAND ON MY SHOULDER...!
THANKS!

P-
PICCOLO?!
N-NO WAY!!
W-WHERE
ARE
YOU?!
PICCOLO
?!!

ANSWER ME,
GOHAN!!
IT'S
PICCOLO!!
QUICKLY!!

I-INTO
MY MIND
...?
YOU CAN ONLY
RESURRECT ONE
OF US WITH EACH
WISH, IS THAT
TRUE?

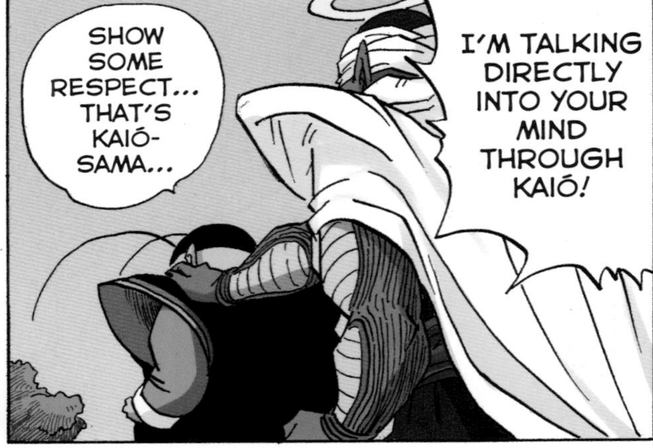
I'M TALKING
DIRECTLY
INTO YOUR
MIND
THROUGH
KAIÓ!
SHOW
SOME
RESPECT...
THAT'S
KAIÓ-
SAMA...

YOU MUST
RAISE **ME** WITH
THE FIRST
WISH!!
LISTEN TO ME—WHEN I
COME BACK TO LIFE,
SO WILL THE GOD OF
EARTH! WE'RE AS ONE!
THEN THE DRAGON
BALLS ON EARTH WILL
BE RESTORED, AND YOU
CAN BRING THE OTHERS
BACK TO LIFE!!

O-OH YEAH!! THAT WOULD WORK!!
...?!
IF Y-Y-YOU SAY SO-!!

HMM. VERY CLEVER.
THAT HE IS...
NOW THE SECOND WISH!!

SUMMON ME TO PLANET NAMEK!! I WANT TO FIGHT!! I WANT TO FIGHT ON MY HOME WORLD AGAINST FREEZA—WHO SLAUGHTERED MY PEOPLE!!
I'VE GAINED GREAT POWER IN THE UNDERWORLD!! I WILL DEFEAT HIM!! TAKE ME THERE!

O-OKAY, PICCOLO!
DO WHAT YOU WILL WITH THE THIRD WISH!

IT'LL BE GOOD TO HAVE YOU WITH US!
H-HEY!! LET'S GET THOSE TWO WISHES MADE!!

DENDE!! ASK HIM TO BRING THE NAMEKIAN ON EARTH CALLED PICCOLO BACK TO LIFE!!
Y-YES... HIS NAME IS PICCOLO, CORRECT?!

YOUR FIRST WISH IS GRANTED.
NOW STATE YOUR SECOND.

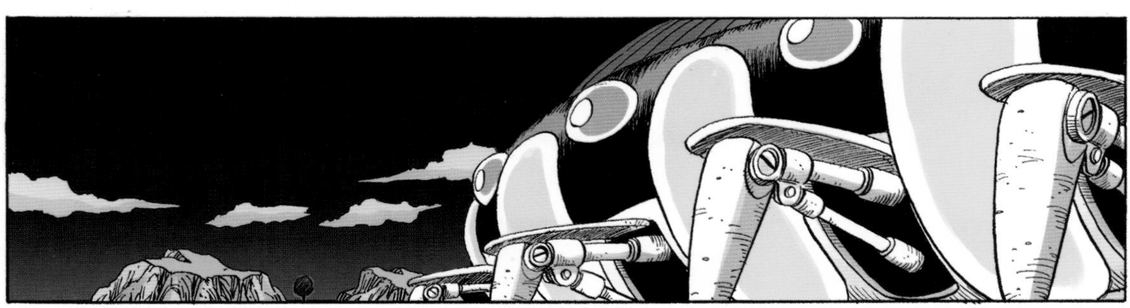

ZZ...
ZZ...

PWIK

SOME-THING'S... COMING CLOSER!!
INCRED-IBLE BATTLE STRENGTH...! IT'S FREEZA!!

B-BUT THIS PLANET HAS MULTIPLE SUNS... IT HAS NO NIGHT...!!
WHAT...?!! THE SKY...IS DARK...?!!

!!

WHAT...IN ALL THE WORLDS ...?!!
!!

A MONSTER ...!!

NO!!

THE DRAGON BALLS ARE GONE!!
AND SO IS KAKAR-ROT'S SON!!

THAT MONSTER MUST BE THE DRAGON THEY WERE TALKING ABOUT...!!

THE LITTLE MAGGOTS ACED ME OUT OF THE WISH!!

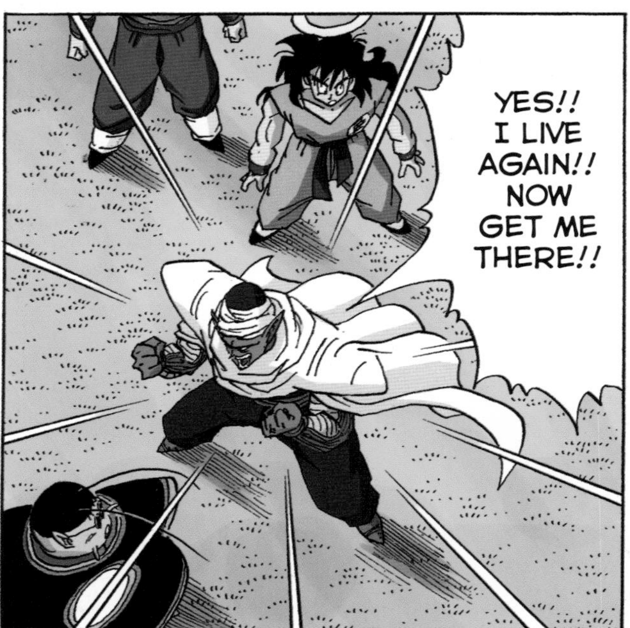

POOF
OH!

HEH... THAT PICCOLO ...
HE DOES THINK QUICKLY ...

K-KAMI-SAMA!!

N-N-NOW TELL HIM TO PLEASE BRING PICCOLO TO PLANET NAMEK!! FAST!!
REALLY?! O-OKAY!!

!!

DENDE, HURRY!! VEGETA'S COMING!!
AAA !!

AH. AN EASY ONE FOR A CHANGE.

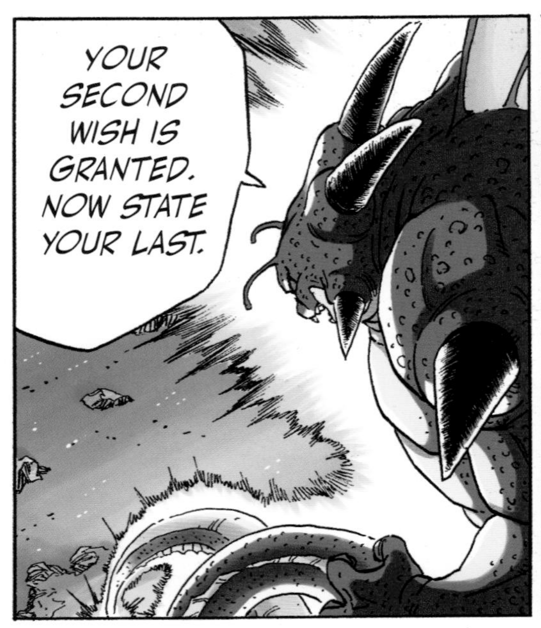
YOUR SECOND WISH IS GRANTED. NOW STATE YOUR LAST.

PFF
OH MY!!

I-I-I ONLY ASKED TO BRING HIM TO THIS PLANET, LIKE YOU SAID...
Y-YOU MEAN YOU WANTED HIM TO COME RIGHT HERE?!

G-GRANTED...? H-HE'S NOT HERE!!
P-PICCOLO, WHERE ARE YOU?!

!!
タッ

AW, NO WAY!!

I SHOULD HAVE KNOWN...!!

WELL, THIS... WILL BE THE LAST BETRAYAL OF YOUR SHORT LIVES!!

WHAT'S THAT PILLAR OF LIGHT?!

THERE'S A LIFE READING THERE!!

NO!! THEY'VE CALLED THE DRAGON ...!!

NOW!! MAKE ME IMMORTAL!!
HURRY FOOLS!! FREEZA'S ALMOST UPON US!!

...

I-IF WE GRANT THAT WISH, HE'LL...!!
B-B-BUT WHAT ELSE CAN WE DO...?!! D-DAD'S STILL HURT... WHO ELSE CAN HELP...?!!

SO THIS... IS HOME...

THIS IS PLANET NAMEK...

Chapter 049 • The Last Wish

I FEEL A POWER FAR AWAY...AN ASTONISHING POWER!! IS THIS THE MONSTER CALLED FREEZA...?!

THERE ARE THREE OTHER CHI NEAR IT... ONE MUST BE GOHAN...!

I AWAIT YOUR FINAL WISH.
STATE IT NOW.

WHY ARE YOU DAW-DLING?! SAY IT!!
MAKE ME IMMORTAL NOW!! DO YOU WANT TO BE KILLED BY FREEZA?!!

BUT HE'S A HELLUVA LOT BETTER THAN FREEZA!! DENDE—DO IT!! YOU'VE GOT TO GRANT HIS WISH!!
AARGH!! VEGETA'S EVIL!! HE KILLED MY FRIENDS!! HE COULD KILL US!!

K-KURIRIN... FREEZA'S ALMOST HERE...!!
... N...

YOU'RE A SMART LAD!!
YES—!!

IF...I HAVE TO...

...

A-ALL RIGHT, THEN...

YOU WON'T BE ABLE TO KILL ME NOW, FREEZA!! I'LL WEAR YOU DOWN!! SOMEDAY, SOMEDAY, I'LL DEFEAT YOU!! THEN I WILL RULE THE UNVERSE!!
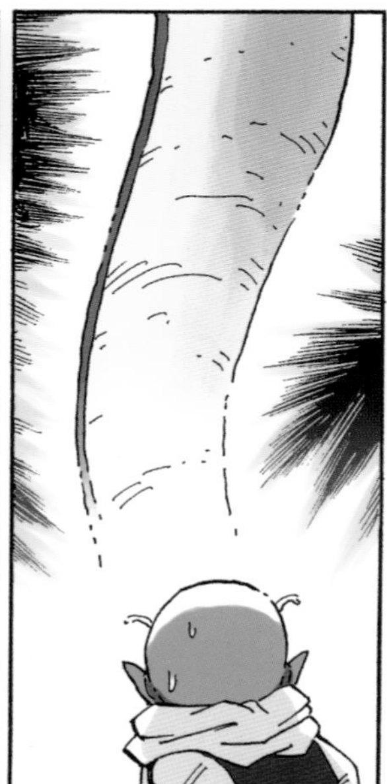

パッ
OH!!

!!

!!!
ドドン

...

W-WHAT HAPPENED HERE...?
WHERE... IS THE DRAGON...? WHERE IS THE NIGHT? W-WHY DID THE DRAGON BALLS TURN TO STONE...?

THE GREAT ELDER... HAS PASSED AWAY...
THE ONE WHO CREATED THE DRAGON BALLS... HAS BEEN CONSUMED BY DEATH AT LAST...

WHAT ABOUT MY WISH?!
WHAT ABOUT MY IMMORTALITY ?!!
I'M SORRY...

YOU DID THIS...YOU CHEATED ME OUT OF EVERY-THING... YOU...

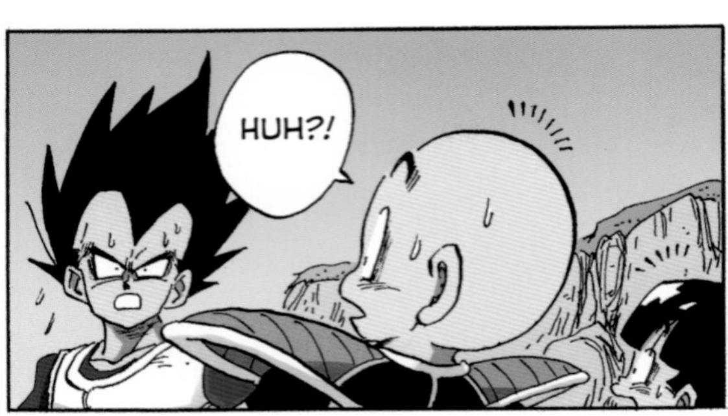
HUH?!

OH... MY...
...
FREEZA!!!

NOW LOOK WHAT YOU'VE DONE...
YOU'VE DESTROYED MY DREAM OF IMMORTALITY...

ぶっ

!!
TMP

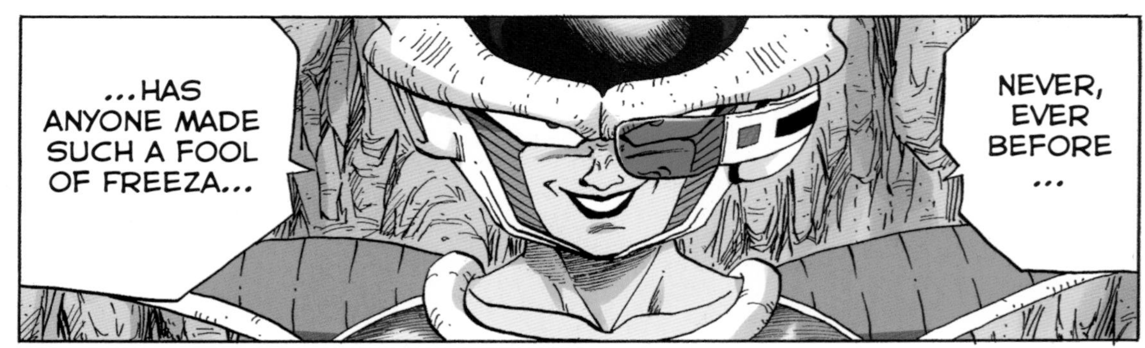
NEVER, EVER BEFORE...
...HAS ANYONE MADE SUCH A FOOL OF FREEZA...

I NEVER THOUGHT I WOULD FACE SUCH A DAY...

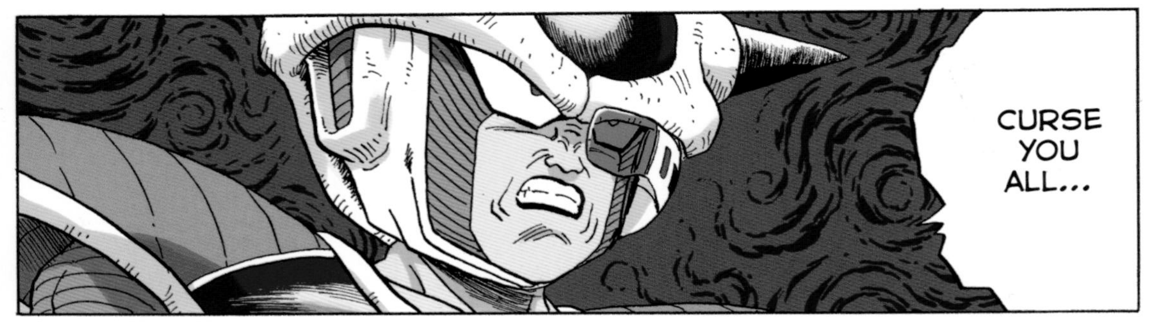

YOU DESPICABLE MAGGOTS!

I'LL TORTURE YOU TO DEATH INCH BY BLOODY INCH!

DON'T TRY TO GET AWAY!!
ババッ

SO MUCH FOR "MY DEAR" AND "*MISTER* VEGETA."
IF YOU THINK I CAN BE BEATEN SO EASILY—THINK AGAIN!!

HEH...OF ALL THE THINGS TO SAY...
HAVE YOU FORGOTTEN WHO I AM...?

LET ME REMIND YOU!!

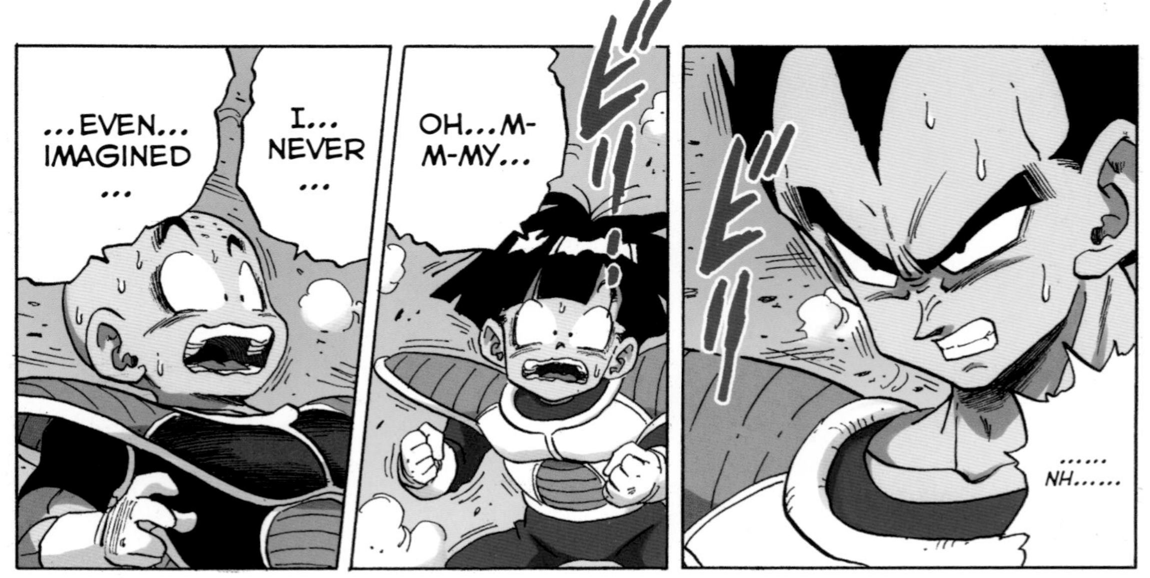
......
NH......
OH...M-
M-MY...
I...
NEVER
...
...EVEN...
IMAGINED
...

THE HUGE CHI WAXES EVEN GREATER!!
FREEZA MUST BE ABOUT TO FIGHT!!!

HM?!

WHAT'S THAT...? ONE VERY WEAK CHI...
THERE'S SOMEONE THERE...!

ダッ

...UH... ...UH...

H-HE LOOKS... JUST LIKE ME...
HE MUST BE NAMEK-IAN...

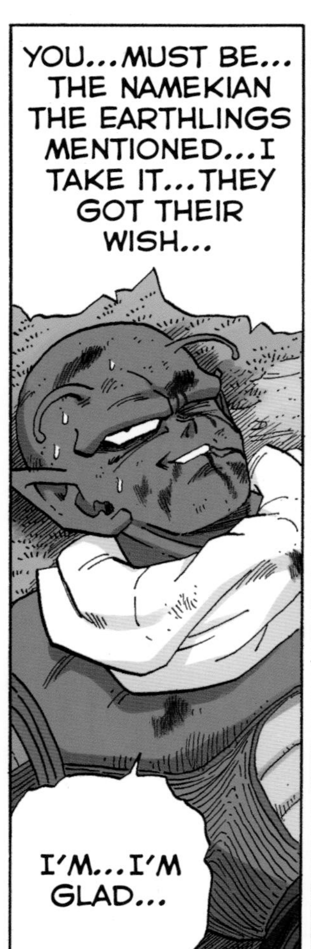
YOU...MUST BE... THE NAMEKIAN THE EARTHLINGS MENTIONED...I TAKE IT...THEY GOT THEIR WISH...
I'M...I'M GLAD...

NOT MUCH LIFE LEFT...

IT'S A PITY... THOUGH...IF YOU WERE TRULY *ONE*... AS A NAMEKIAN... THEN YOU MIGHT BE ABLE TO DEFEAT...EVEN FREEZA...
OF COURSE. I...I DON'T KNOW WHAT SORT OF... TRAINING YOU'VE HAD...BUT... YOU HAVE AN ASTONISHING AMOUNT OF POWER...
WHAT ?!

HMPH... YOU SEEM TO BE FAMILIAR WITH THE DETAILS...
THEN YOU SHOULD ALSO KNOW THAT I'M IN A HURRY TO SAVE THOSE BRATS.
I'M AFRAID I HAVE TO LEAVE YOU HERE TO DIE.

ARE YOU TELLING ME—IF I BECOME ONE WITH *KAMI* AGAIN, THEN I COULD EVEN SURPASS THAT SCOUNDREL FREEZA'S POWER?!

YES...I WAS... UTTERLY CRUSHED BY HIM... BUT I THINK I UNDERSTAND HIS CAPABILITIES...

WELL, THERE'S NOTHING I CAN DO NOW!
AND I HAVE NO DESIRE TO BECOME ONE WITH THAT FOOL AGAIN!

I AM THIS PLANET'S... *ONLY* WARRIOR NAMEKIAN...
THEN... ASSIMI-LATE ME!

W-WHAT?!
WITH YOU?!
YES...YOUR STRENGTH...WILL INCREASE EXPONENTIALLY...

THANKS FOR THE OFFER... BUT NO THANKS!
I DON'T WANT MY PERSONALITY TO BECOME ONE WITH YOU, EITHER! I WANT TO BE ME!

THERE'S...NO TIME...I WILL SOON DIE...HURRY...AND PUT YOUR HAND ON MY BODY...
DON'T WORRY...YOUR PERSONALITY WILL BE YOUR OWN...I WILL MERELY BE... THE CATA-LYST...

...
YOU'D BETTER NOT BE LYING...
IF YOU THINK I AM...GO AHEAD... GO JUST AS YOU ARE NOW...AND SEE HOW YOU FARE AGAINST FREEZA...

...

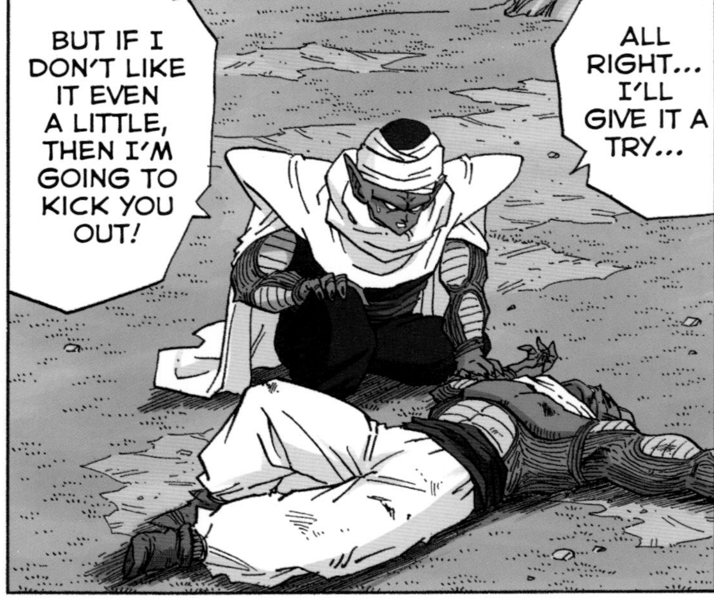
ALL RIGHT... I'LL GIVE IT A TRY...
BUT IF I DON'T LIKE IT EVEN A LITTLE, THEN I'M GOING TO KICK YOU OUT!

I THINK ONLY... OF NAMEK...AND THE UNIVERSE. I HOPE...YOU WILL TOO...
I'M IN A HURRY! GET ON WITH IT!

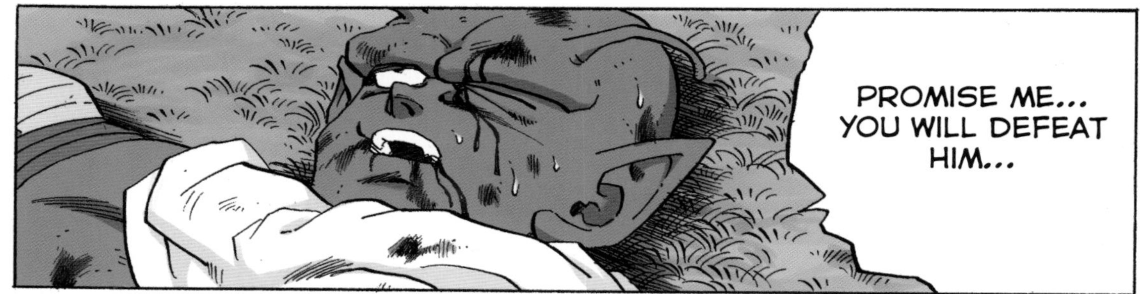
PROMISE ME... YOU WILL DEFEAT HIM...

YOU DON'T HAVE TO ASK.
I WANT TO DO IT FOR MYSELF.

HEH...

UNH!!

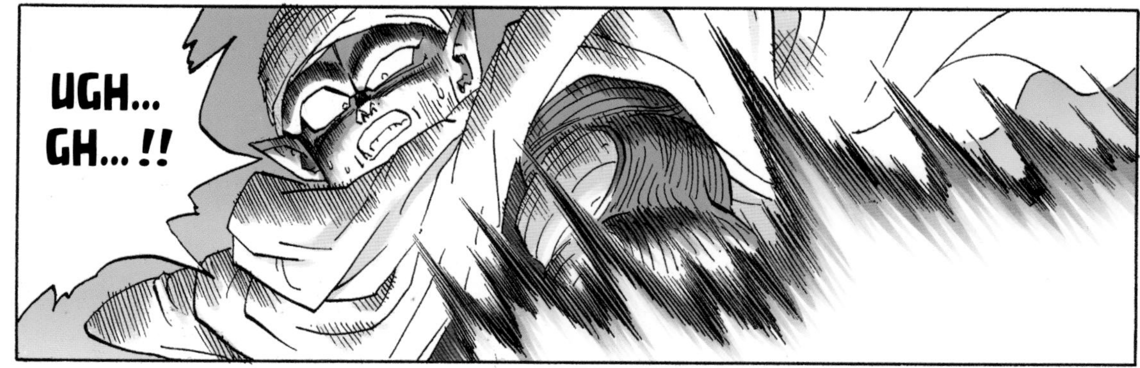
UGH... GH...!!

HUFF
HUGH

...

SUCH AWESOME... INCOMPRE-HENSIBLE POWER...!!

THIS POWER ...!!

SO THIS IS ASSIMILA-TION ...!!

HA HA
HA!!

...
ガタガタ...

HIS POWER'S TOO HIGH...
TH-THERE'S NO WAY WE CAN BEAT HIM...!

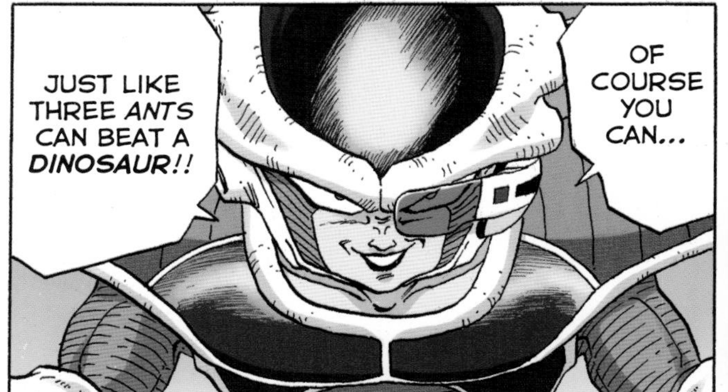
OF COURSE YOU CAN...
JUST LIKE THREE *ANTS* CAN BEAT A ***DINOSAUR!!***

WE CAN BEAT HIM!
WITH ALL THREE OF US—I KNOW WE CAN!!

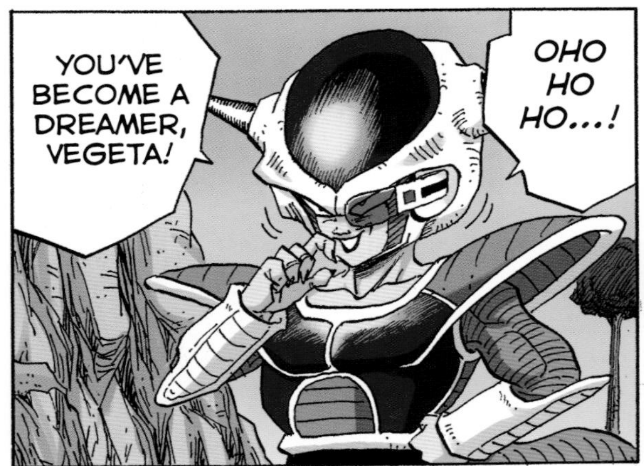
OHO HO HO...!
YOU'VE BECOME A DREAMER, VEGETA!

WHAT?
HUH?!

NONE OF YOU SEEMS TO HAVE REALIZED...
HOW THESE EARTHLINGS' BATTLE STRENGTHS KEEP RISING! THE YOUNG ONE HAS POWERS IN HIM HE CAN'T EVEN DREAM OF!

WHILE I, FREEZA, SLOWLY BECOME WHAT YOU DREAD MOST... THE *SUPER SAIYAN*...!!

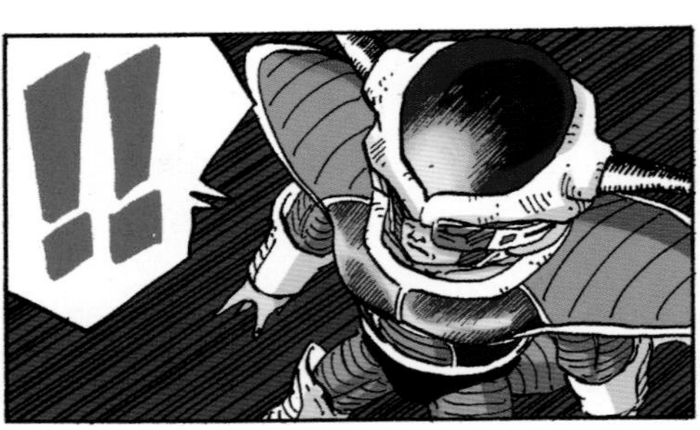
!!

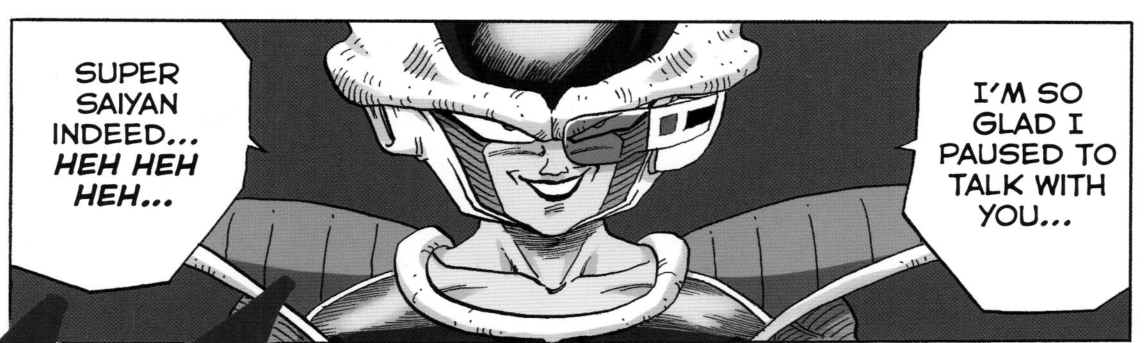
SUPER SAIYAN INDEED... *HEH HEH HEH...*
I'M SO GLAD I PAUSED TO TALK WITH YOU...

NOW YOU DIE!!!

NN...
NNNH...!!

pii pii pii pii pii pii

piii...
WHAT ?!

A...AAH...!!

!!
BOM

I SEE...
SO YOU WEREN'T ENTIRELY BLUFF-ING...

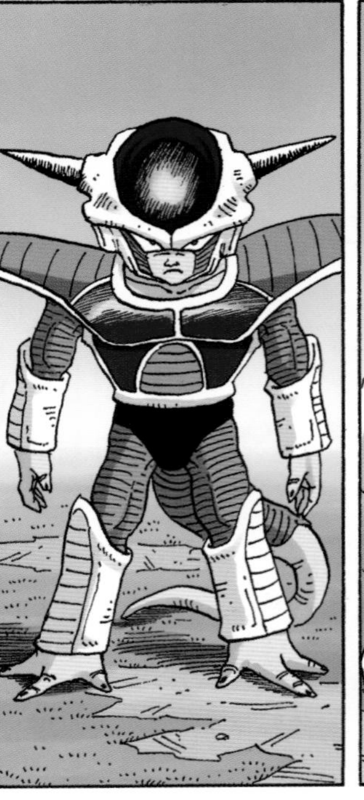

huff
huff

H-HE'S RIGHT...!! IF WE FIGHT TOGETHER... MAYBE WE C-COULD DO IT...!!
HE'S AWESOME... B-BUT OUR STRENGTH HAS INCREASED...!

B-BUT THEN... W-WHY IS FREEZA SO CALM...?
Y-YEAH...!! IT'S LIKE...VEGETA'S BR-BROKEN THROUGH ANOTHER POWER CEILING, Y'KNOW...?!

YOU MIGHT AS WELL TRANSFORM *NOW*—AND SHOW US WHAT YOU *REALLY* ARE!
TRANSFORM, FREEZA!

YOUR FRIEND ZARBON WASN'T THE MOST DISCREET.
I AM SURPRISED YOU KNOW. HOW DID YOU FIND OUT?
HM!

IF YOU WANT IT SO MUCH... I'LL SHOW YOU!!
ALL RIGHT ...!!

TR...

TRANS-FORM ...?!

Chapter 051 • The Transformation

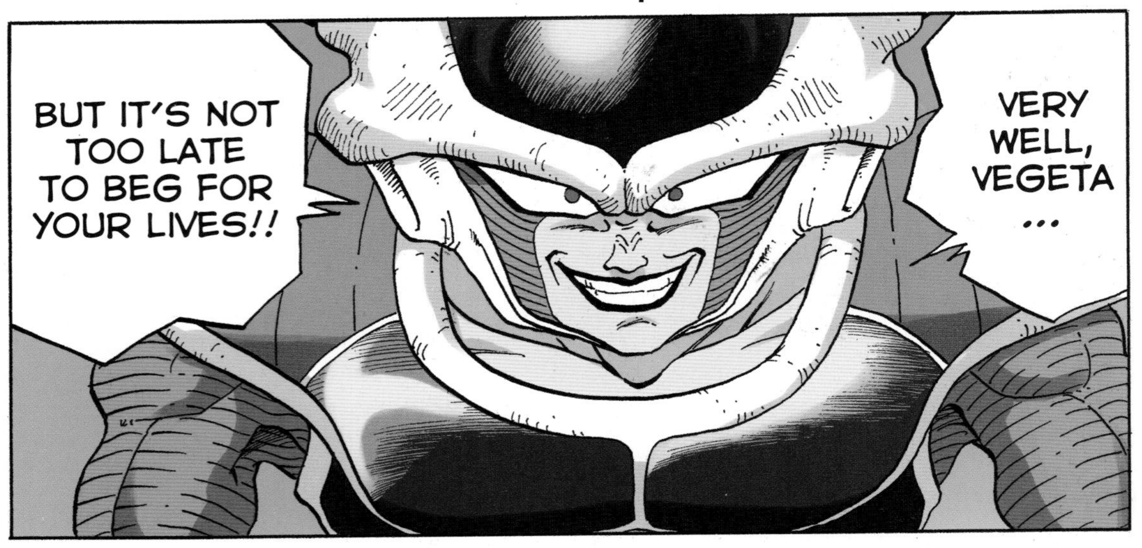

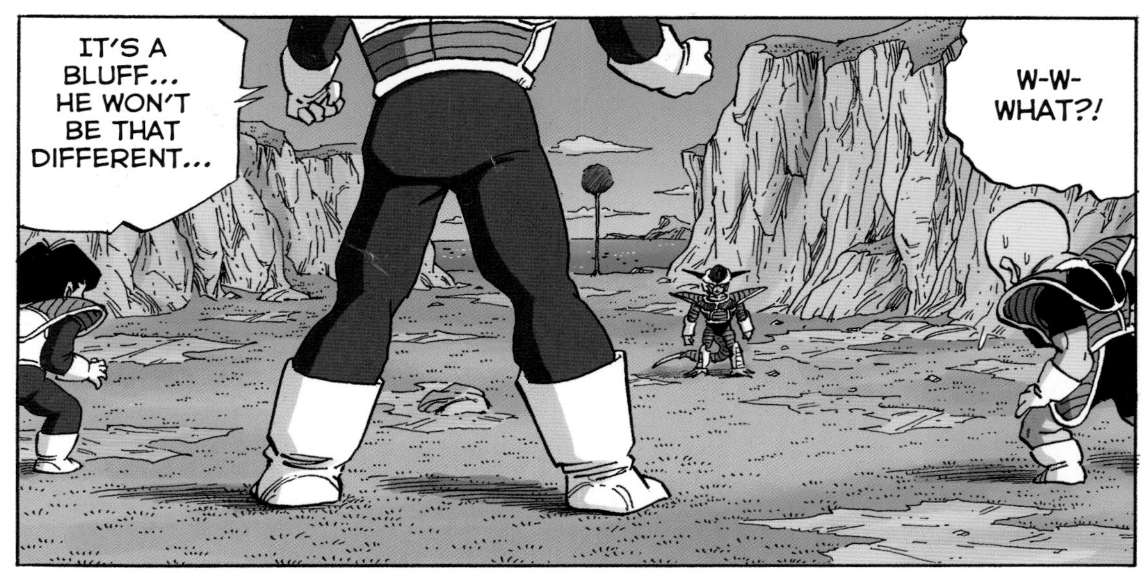

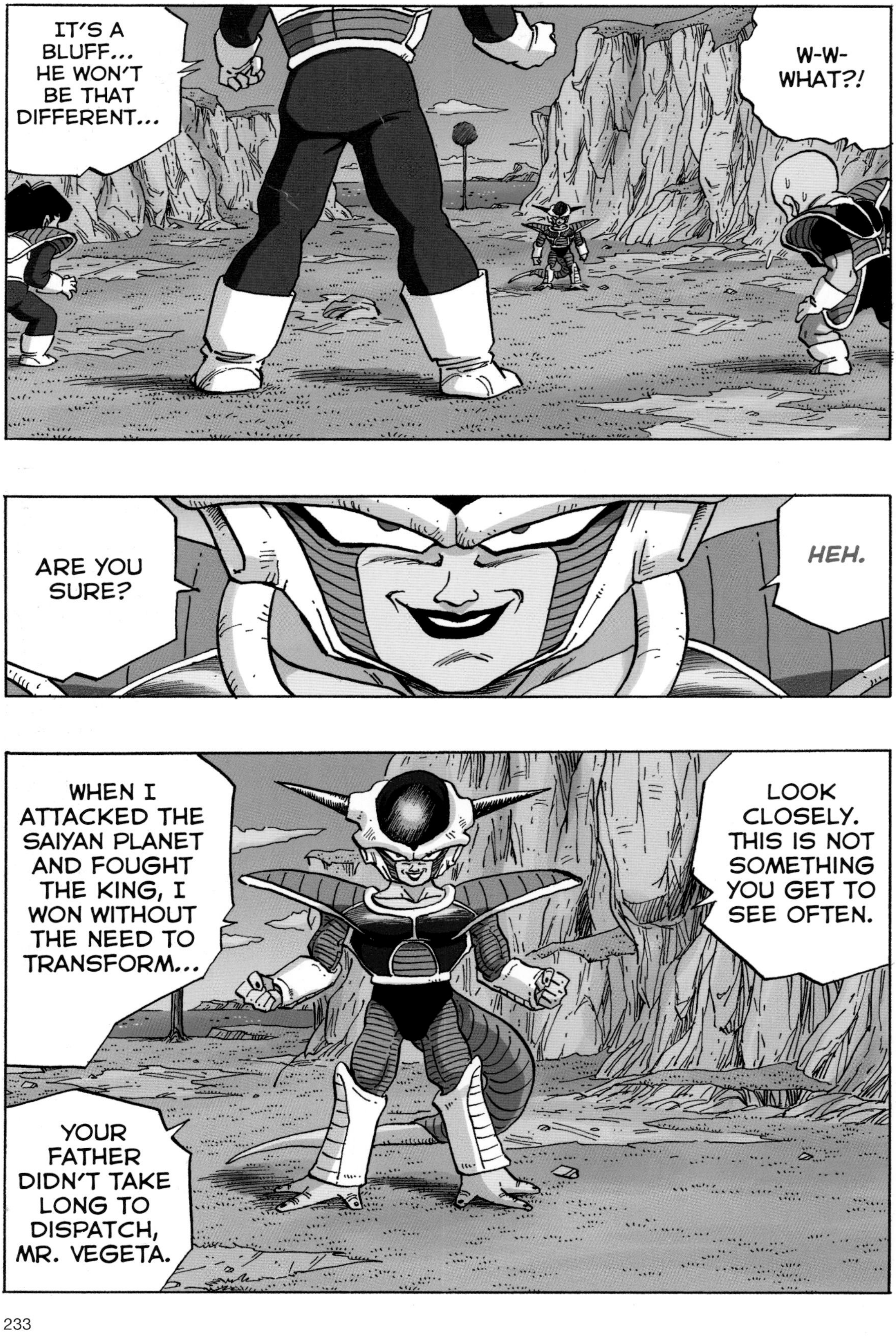

LOOK CLOSELY. THIS IS NOT SOMETHING YOU GET TO SEE OFTEN.

WHEN I ATTACKED THE SAIYAN PLANET AND FOUGHT THE KING, I WON WITHOUT THE NEED TO TRANSFORM...

YOUR FATHER DIDN'T TAKE LONG TO DISPATCH, MR. VEGETA.

S-SO THE SAIYAN PLANET... WAS DESTROYED BY HIM...?!

FEH...!
DON'T GET ALL HIGH AND MIGHTY OVER *THAT*...I HAD ALREADY SURPASSED HIM WHEN I WAS A KID!

EEK

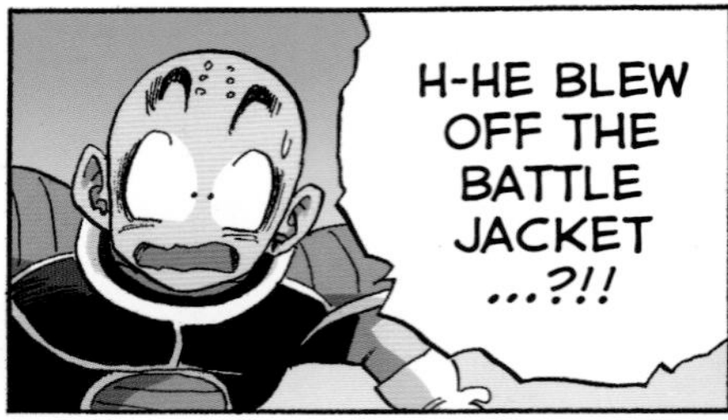
H-HE BLEW OFF THE BATTLE JACKET ...?!!

OH, NO! THE MIGHTY FREEZA TOOK OFF HIS JACKET!
IS THAT THE GREAT "TRANS-FORMA-TION"?!

HEH

ブル
ブル
ブル

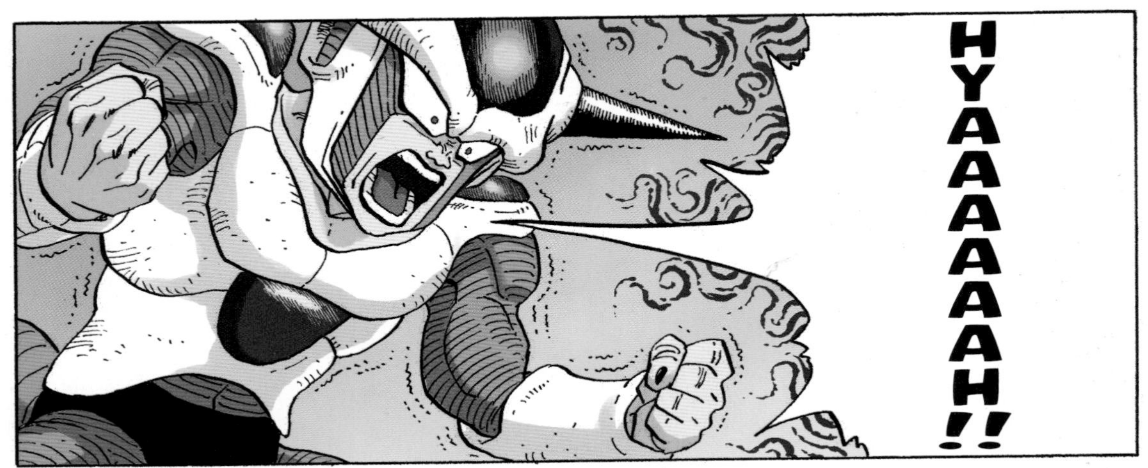
HYAAAAAAH!!

UH-OH...
H-HIS *CHI* IS GETTING STRONGER...!!

!!

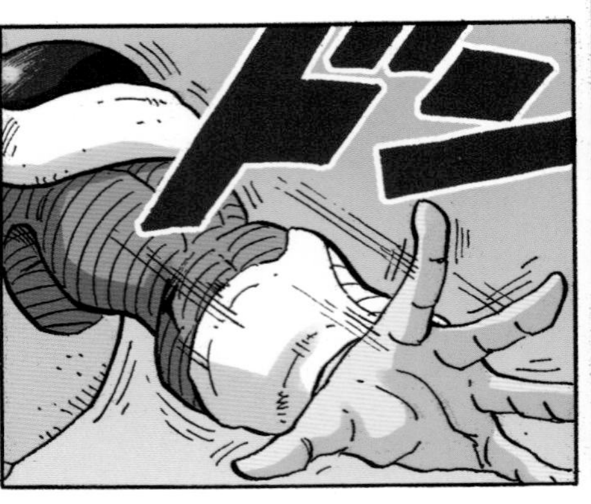

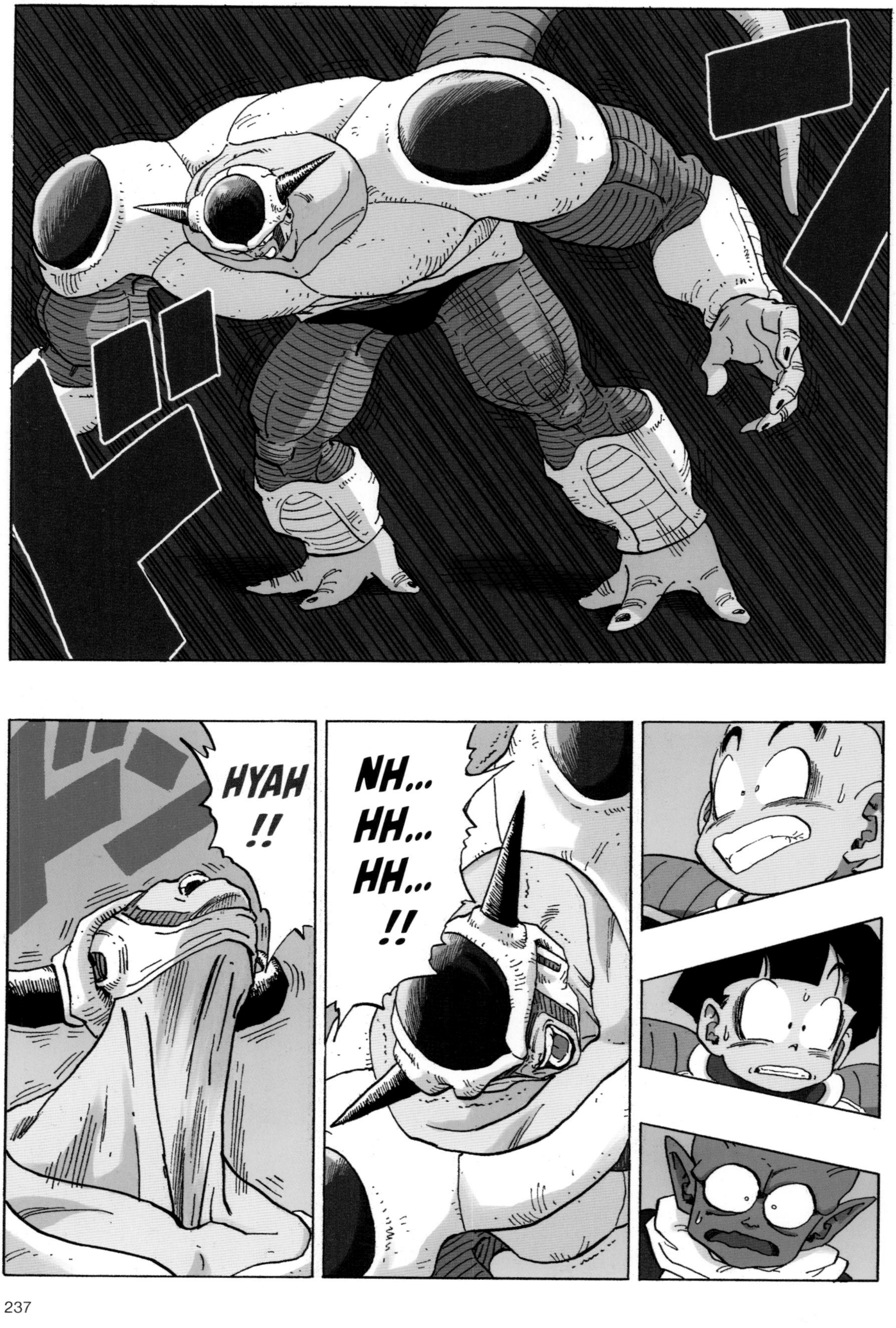

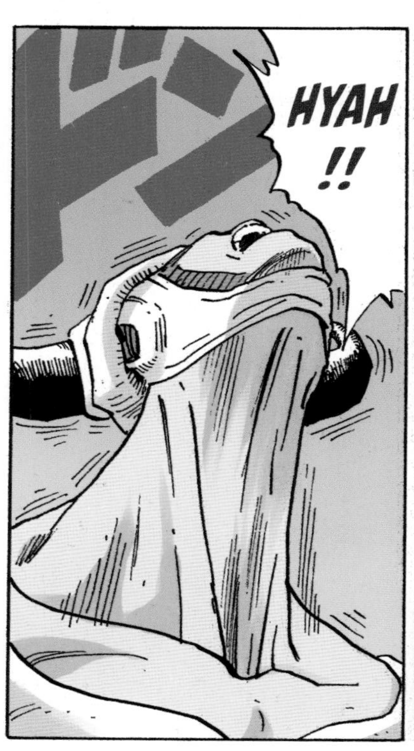
HYAH
!!
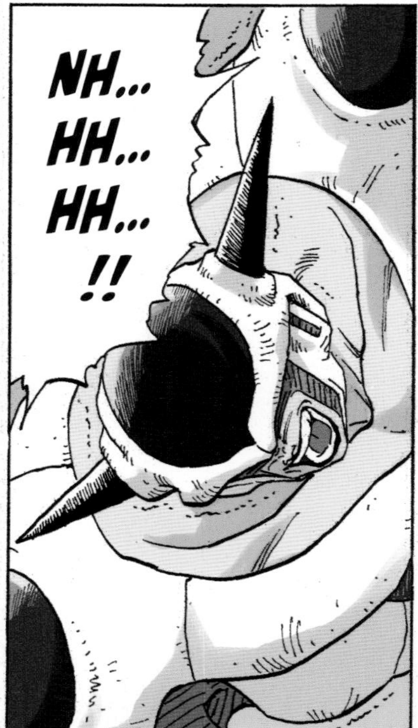
NH...
HH...
HH...
!!

HUHH
HUHH

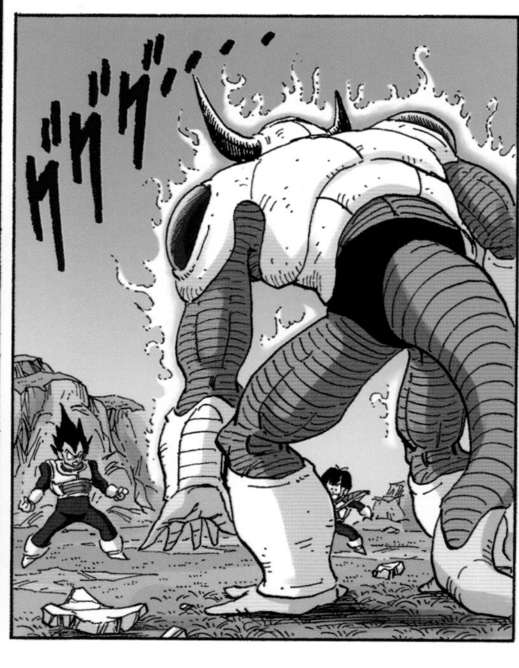

HEH HEH HEH... WATCH OUT...

I WON'T BE AS GENTLE AS I WAS BEFORE...

I HAVE SO MUCH POWER NOW...I MIGHT NOT BE ABLE TO CONTROL IT...

IF ANY INSTRUMENT COULD READ MY STRENGTH... IT WOULD SURPASS A MILLION...

BAH!!

YAAA!!

UNH
!!

ズザザザ…
...!!

W-
WHERE'S
KURIRIN
...?!!
A-AND
DENDE
...?!!

HA HA HA. YOU'RE ALL PRETTY QUICK ON YOUR FEET, AS I EXPECTED.

OF COURSE, THAT WAS NOTHING. EVEN ***SAIYANS*** COULD DO THAT.

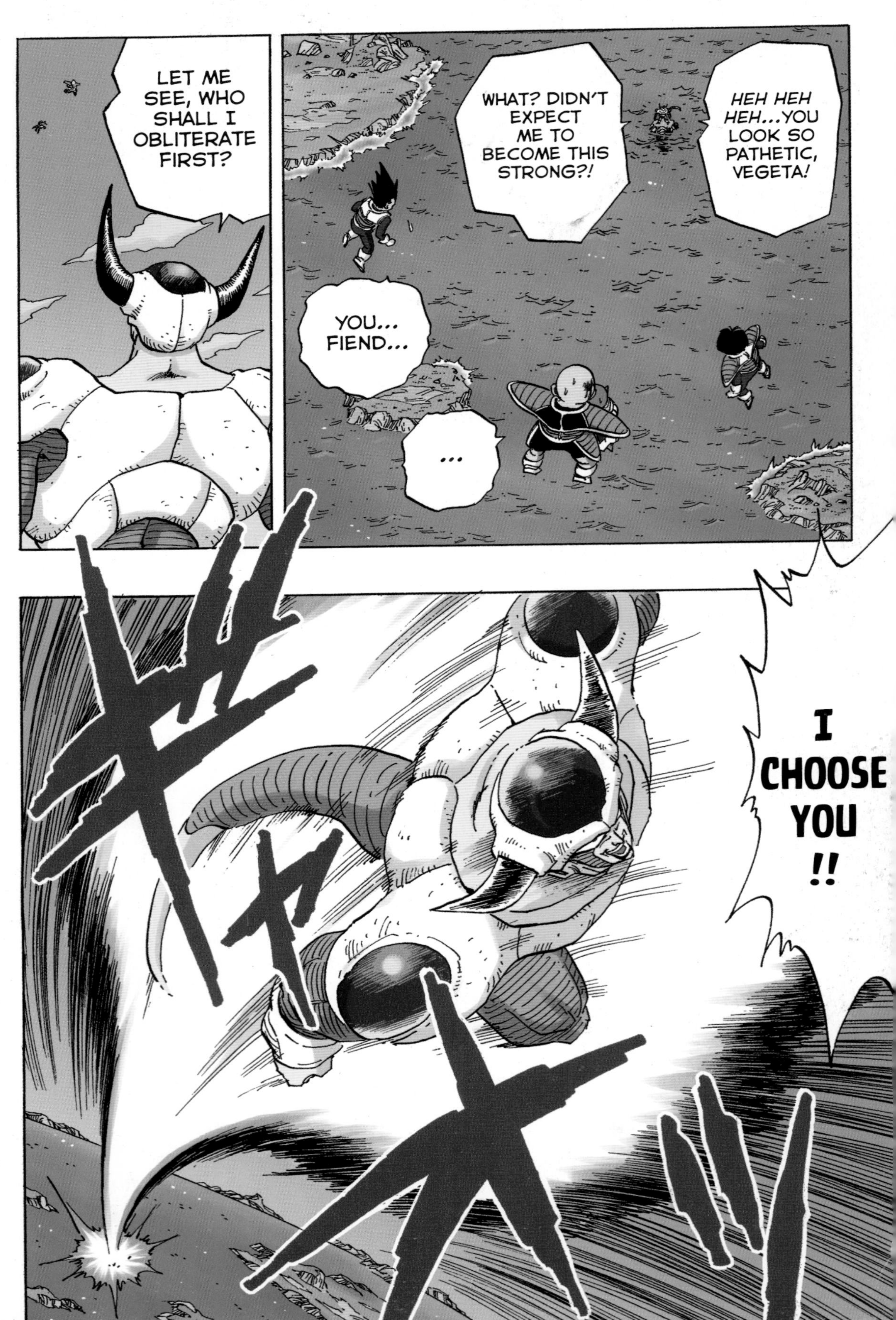

HEH HEH HEH...YOU LOOK SO PATHETIC, VEGETA!
WHAT? DIDN'T EXPECT ME TO BECOME THIS STRONG?!
YOU... FIEND...
...
LET ME SEE, WHO SHALL I OBLITERATE FIRST?
I CHOOSE YOU!!

GAH !!

T-TOO FAST !!

KURIRIN!!

AKIRA TORIYAMA

Renowned worldwide for his playful, innovative storytelling and humorous, distinctive art style, Akira Toriyama burst onto the manga scene in 1980 with the wildly popular ***Dr. Slump***. His hit series ***Dragon Ball*** (published in the U.S. as ***Dragon Ball*** and ***Dragon Ball Z***) ran from 1984 to 1995 in Shueisha's ***Weekly Shonen Jump*** magazine. He is also known for his design work on video games such as ***Dragon Quest***, ***Chrono Trigger***, ***Tobal No. 1*** and ***Blue Dragon***. His recent manga works include ***COWA!***, ***Kajika***, ***Sand Land***, ***Neko Majin***, ***Toccio the Angel*** and ***Jaco the Galactic Patrolman***. He lives with his family in Japan.

SOUND EFFECTS GLOSSARY

The sound effects in this color edition of Dragonball have been preserved in their original Japanese format. To avoid additional lettering cluttering up the panels, a list of the sound effects (FX) is provided here. Each FX is listed by page and panel number, so for example 6.4 would mean the FX is on page 6 in panel 4. If there is a third number, it means there is more than one FX in the panel—214.1.1 and 214.1.2 for example.

31.3 VII—IIN
36.2 SSHH
36.2 VNNN
36.3 VOOSH
37.1 BAMM
37.2 WOOM BWAM
37.2 VMMM
37.3 BM BM BM
37.3 SHP SHP
38.1 VIP
39.1 BWAK
39.2 VOOOSH
40.1 TOOM
41.1 GYOOOOOM
41.2 BOK
42.1 THUDD
43.5 FLASSSSH
44.2 SSHH
44.3 PWOK
44.5 TM
45.1 D OOM
45.3 ZA-BOOM
46.1 TTTMMM
47.4/3 KIII—IIN
53.1 HOOOON HOOOON
55.6 KIIIIIN
59.5 ZOOM ZOOM
61.1 DOOOOSH
62.1 WAK
62.2 DOOOM
63.1 WHRRRRR

6.4 HYA
7.1 HO HA
7.3 YA
7.4 VIIIIN
8.2 VOOOSH
9.2 GLARE
11.5 GRRR RRR
12.5 HYA
13.2 HWOOOO
14.2 DOM
15.3 WOBBLE WOBBLE
15.4 TOOM
21.1 VM VM
21.2 VYOO VYOO
22.1 SHFF SHFF
22.3 SMACK
23.1 FOOSH
23.3 DK DK
24.1 VISH
24.2 SHAP
24.3 BM BM
25.3 WHSH
26.1 DO OM
26.2/3 WOOSH
27.1 SKRIII
27.2 SKRIII
29.3 VMMM
29.5 BAM
30.2 VWOOOSH
30.5 BAP
31.1 VWO OOSH

93.3	SHK
93.4	RRRRMMMM
95.4	DOOM
96.2	HWOG
97.1	GNG
97.2	G-G-G-G
97.5	KRAK
98.2	THOG
99.2	ZHOOP
101.6	DOOSH
102.1	GLOOB
102.4	BZ ZZT
108.1	HYUUUN HYUUUN
110.3	VYOOON VYOOON
118.3	KIIIIIN
118.4	SHP SHP
123.5	BWAK
124.2	TUP
127.1	SHOOM
128.1	VNNNN
128.2	BAM BAM BAM
129.1	BMM BMM BMM
132.5	THWAK
134.1	WHOK
134.2	KONG
134.3	SKRIII
135.1	BOWW
135.2	SHP
135.3	DOM
136.4	VOON
136.5	SPAP SPAP
136.5	BAM BWAP
137.1	VIIII
137.2	WAK
137.3	D-BAM-BAM
138.2	BWAK
138.7	KRNCH
139.4	WH AK
140.1	ZOOOOM
140.2	BWUK
63.2	VNNN
63.3	SHF
63.3	ZIP
63.4	POW POW POW
63.4	VWOOOOO
63.4	SHP SHP SHP
64.1	FWA FWA
64.2	TM
64.3	TM
65.2	KIIIIN
67.1	ZWOOO
68.1	FWAA
68.1/2	HOOSH
68.3	BWOOOM
69.1	VOOOOO
69.2	PING
69.3	SLASH
70.2	KRAK
70.3	BM BM BM BM
70.3	KRAK WHAK
71.1	FWASH
71.2	HIIIII
72.1	FWAAA
72.3	GUMP
73.5	ZPP
75.4	RRRRMMMM
76.2	RRRRMMMM
77.1	SSHHH...
78.1	SHH...
81.2	KIIIIIN
82.3	ZHOOO
83.4	VOOON
84.3	VYOOOON
85.1	KRIII
87.6	PIIP
88.1	DOOM
88.3	SSSS
91.3	HYUUUUN HYUUUUN
92.1	KIIIII—N

205.3 VVV
205.4 VIIIIIN
208.1 KYOOOO
208.3 PFFT
209.1 D-MM D-MM
213.1 SSS
215.1 VSSH
216.1 RRRMMMM
216.2 MMM
216.3 MMM
217.1 KIII—N
217.4 TP
221.4 VOOSH
221.5 HYOOOO
222.1 FYOOOO
224.1 HOOOSH
224.2 VNNNN
225.1 SSSHHH
225.3 RRRM RRRM
227.2 DO OM
228.1 KR AK
228.2 GGGGG...
229.1 WAK
229.2 RRRRMMM
230.1 VSH
234.3 BOOM
235.5 RRR RRR RRR
236.3 DOOM
236.5 DOOM
237.1 DO OM
237.6 DOOM
239.1 NNNGG
241.1 HOOSH
242.1 BA-BOOM
242.3 PATTA PATTA
243.3 SHOOSH
244.3 VOOSH
245.1 TNG
141.4 DO OM
143.1 VNNNN
143.2 FSH
143.3 DDNK
144.1 BWAK
144.2 VNNN
144.3 TH OK
145.1 VN NN
145.3 WAM
146.1 DKOOM
146.5 FSH
147.1 NVVV
148.1 VNN—--N
149.2 BAM
149.3 VMMM
150.2 B ZAK
151.3 TMP
153.5 FSH
155.1 GNG
156.1 B ZAK
157.1 PLAP
165.1 VYOOOO
166.3 VSH
167.1 DOOM
168.2 VVV
168.3 SHF
168.4 WHAK
170.3 DOOM
173.1 KYOOOO
174.3 KIII—N
175.1 GYUUUUN
179.4 TIP TOE—
181.1-3 DOOOOM
182.3 MMMMM
183.2 PSSHHHH
184.1 WOOOONNN
186.1 RRRMMMM...
191.4 TUP
200.6 TMP
202.2 VOOOONNN

DRAGON BALL FULL COLOR FREEZA ARC Volume 3

SHONEN JUMP Edition

STORY & ART BY **AKIRA TORIYAMA**

Translation **Mari Morimoto**
English Adaptation **Gerard Jones**
Lettering **Zack Turner**
Cover & Interior Design **Shawn Carrico**
Editor **Mike Montesa**

Printed in China

Published by VIZ Media, LLC
P.O. Box 77010
San Francisco, CA 94107

10 9 8 7 6 5 4 3 2 1
First printing, September 2016